To Basil Pennington, O.C.S.O.

LIVING WORDS

A Simple Study of Key New Testament Concepts
for People Who Don't Know a Word of Greek

Anthony E. Gilles

Nihil Obstat:
>   Rev. Hilarion Kistner, O.F.M.
>   Rev. John J. Jennings

Imprimi Potest:
>   Rev. Jeremy Harrington, O.F.M.
>   Provincial

Imprimatur:
>   †James H. Garland, V.G.
>   Archdiocese of Cincinnati
>   August 13, 1985

The *nihil obstat* and *imprimatur* are a declaration that a book or pamphlet is considered to be free from doctrinal or moral error. It is not implied that those who have granted the *nihil obstat* and *imprimatur* agree with the content, opinions or statements expressed.

Book design and cover by Julie Lonneman.

SBN 0-86716-051-9

©1985, Anthony E. Gilles
All rights reserved
Published by St. Anthony Messenger Press
Printed in the U.S.A.

Errata
>   The page numbering of this book mistakenly skips from page 69 to page 80. No text, however, is omitted and all references to page numbers within the text, the Locater Chart and the Indexes correspond to this existing pagination.

Contents

Introduction

Words are fascinating creatures. Through them we are able
to communicate with each other and share who we really
are—the depths of our values, aspirations and dreams. God
shares with us in this same way: through the words of
Scripture revealed to us through human authors. The Word
of God in Scripture (God's *rhema*, see p. 120) comes to
us through the ordinary words of human language. Insofar
as the New Testament is concerned, those ordinary words
were first written in Greek.

Since few of us read Greek, we come to know God's
revealed Word by reading English translations of the original
Greek Scriptures. Such translations are, of course, a great
blessing, since without them Scripture's meaning would
be lost to most of us. Nonetheless, if we want to understand
what the New Testament writers really meant by what they
wrote, we have to read their writings on *their* terms, not our
own. And to do this we must come to at least a minimal
appreciation of the language in which they wrote—Greek.

Luke and John and the other evangelists didn't have
crystal balls before them when they wrote. They didn't know
how *we* would translate *their* words. It was not their
responsibility to make sure that their Greek words came
across clearly in our 20th-century idiom. Rather, it is *our*
responsibility to go back to their words and measure our
understandings against them so that these New Testament
words are fully significant for us today.

That is the purpose of this book: to help us understand
more fully what the New Testament authors meant by the
Greek words they used. To put it another way, the purpose

1

of this book is to help the New Testament writers communicate better with us today.

A Word About Translations

You may be asking yourself at this point if there aren't several excellent modern translations of the Greek New Testament into contemporary English. Indeed there are. The four best are the *New American Bible* (NAB), *The New International Version* (NIV), *The New English Bible* (NEB) and *The Jerusalem Bible* (JB). Why not just rely on these excellent translations? Why go beyond the work the translators have already done?

This question does not take into account how translations of the Bible come into existence. Someone does not hand Luke's original Greek Gospel to a famous scholar and say, "Here, Mortimer, change all this Greek into words that the 'now-generation' will understand." It doesn't work like that.

In the first place, Luke's "original Greek manuscript" does not exist. There are handwritten copies of his original (or parts of it) which the translators must first read in order to decide what Luke himself actually wrote. What if one copy of a Gospel manuscript has an entire sentence that another copy lacks? This is actually the case, for example, with Lk 23:17: "At the festival he [Pilate] had to release a prisoner to them" is a verse which is found in some ancient copies but missing in others. The first step in "translation," therefore, is to decide which ancient copy (or copies) of an original manuscript to use.

No one person could both sort out all the copies and at the same time make a completely new translation. That would be terribly laborious and time-consuming. So translators today work in teams—and there is by *no* means unanimity among team members as to certain points of translation.

As an example, consider an incident related to me by a famous scholar who served on a team which translated Mark's Gospel for one of today's modern English versions. At one point during a "discussion" over the team's translation, one member stood up and shouted to another, "You're not *translating,* you're *interpreting,* and I'll be damned if I'm going to continue working on this project!" The aggrieved scholar then stalked out of the room and never returned.

While this story is an isolated and no doubt atypical example of how modern Bible translators carry on their work, it illustrates my point that unanimity among Bible scholars (or any other scholars, for that matter) is nonexistent. The truth is that reasonable and highly educated people can and do have honest differences of opinion. Thus to "go beyond the translators' work" in order to get a feel for the original Greek will enhance the value of the modern translations. Our purpose is not to challenge the scholars' achievement, but to see for ourselves how rich and varied the original Greek is, and how helpful an understanding of the original Greek is to the entire sense and purpose of Scripture.

Without that understanding, we can't be sure that we know precisely what the New Testament writers meant when we read today's English translations. For example, the translators of the *King James Version,* writing in the 16th century, defined faith as "the substance of things hoped for, the evidence of things not seen" (Heb 11:1). The translators of the *New American Bible,* 400 years later, defined faith as "confident assurance concerning what we hope for, and conviction about things we do not see." Are the two definitions equivalent? Not exactly. In order to understand the distinction we must analyze the Greek words actually used in Heb 11:1 (which we do on p. 114).

We could give many more examples of the vagaries of translated Greek words, and we do precisely that in the pages ahead. Often, however, we will find that our study in this book will not reveal discrepancies in translations so much as it will call us to recover the riches of words and concepts whose translations from the Greek have *not* varied with time. For words grown familiar lose freshness and impact.

For example, the words *atonement, compassion* and *forgiveness*—no matter how one translates the Greek—still

3

come out pretty much the same in today's English. But do we really appreciate the root meaning of these words? Do we realize that *atonement* is literally "at-one-ment," a state of being in union with someone? Do we understand that *com-passion* suggests "to suffer with" someone, or that *forgiveness* connotes a favorable disposition toward giving without counting the cost?

We will find in the pages ahead that, as we explore the Greek words underlying our English translations, we will at the same time come to a deeper understanding of the English words themselves. As we go back to the Greek and strip away layers of age and dust, we restore power to familiar English words and concepts. And *that*, after all, is the whole purpose of reading Scripture in the first place: to encounter the *power* of God's Word, that "sword of the spirit" (Eph 6:17), that gospel "leading everyone who believes in it to salvation" (Rom 1:16).

Before continuing, let me stress one point. You do not have to *know* Greek in order to understand this book, nor will you have to *learn* Greek anywhere along the way. Some of you may want to pursue a study of Greek after reading this book and, if you do, so much the better. For those of you so inclined, I have provided an Appendix at the end of this book which briefly explains Greek grammar, enough to give you a taste for the subject.

For now, however, *"me phobon, monon pisteue"* ("Fear not, only believe," Mk 5:36). There. You've just read a Greek sentence and lived to tell about it!

A Word About Greek

Greek has acquired a rather bad name. It's true that it is a difficult language to learn, but it's not as difficult as our prejudiced attitudes against this beautiful and melodious language would indicate.

Perhaps it's that funny-looking alphabet which scares people away from the study of Greek. You will notice in the Greek phrase I quoted above that I used the ordinary English alphabet. The table on p. 137 offers a brief look at the Greek alphabet—for simplicity's sake, only the lower-case

4

letters—and the sounds for which the letters stand.

But, for our purposes, there is no need to learn this alphabet. In the first place, this is not the form of the Greek alphabet actually used by the New Testament authors. I won't even attempt to draw the ancient Greek characters. Suffice it to say that if you could see first-century Greek handwriting, your reaction would greatly exceed the cliche, "It's all Greek to me!"

Furthermore, in the pages ahead I will *transliterate* that alphabet for you into our English alphabet. For example, instead of writing Ιησους I will write *Iesous* (Jesus); instead of writing Χωρα, I will write *chora* (country).

Now, let's talk about pronunciation. There are two ways we could proceed. One would be to train you to pronounce every word like a Greek master—in effect to turn you into another Demosthenes. To accomplish this I would have to put in all sorts of accent marks, pronunciation codes and English equivalents. The result would resemble a hieroglyphic slab removed from King Tut's tomb. I somehow think you are not quite that interested in pronouncing Greek to perfection.

I have chosen the simpler approach. I will give guides to pronunciation only for the *key* words we will study. (We will put these English equivalents right after the English translation of the key Greek word.) This means that you will not know how to pronounce perfectly every single Greek word in the upcoming text. If that's all right with you, it's all right with me.

My purpose in this book is not to train you to *pro-nounce* Greek to perfection, but to enable you to come to grips on a rudimentary level with the *meaning* of the Greek. If you slip up on pronouncing some of the words, don't worry about it.

Let's look, for example, at a commonly mispronounced Greek word. You've probably seen the word *logos* (from Jn 1:1, meaning "Word"). Most people pronounce it "low-goes," which is incorrect. It's actually pronounced "law-gaws." But for our purposes here, does it make a great deal of difference how we pronounce it? The main purpose behind our study of *logos* (see page 91) will be to help you understand the *significance* of *logos* to the New Testament writers. We're not out to win any Greek pronunciation contests.

Therefore, in the pages ahead, to simplify your study of the *meaning* of the Greek words, I have tried to keep you from getting bogged down in a study of Greek pronunciation. To master meaning *and* pronunciation in the same book would make for difficult reading. So, if I were you I wouldn't try to impress my friends by holding forth on the correct pronunciation of New Testament Greek verbs. Simply dazzle them with your new understanding of the meaning of New Testament Greek and let it go at that.

Finally, you will notice that many of the Greek sentences I quote in the pages ahead don't start with capital letters. That is because I take the words directly from the Greek sentences in which they are found, and in most cases the quoted words come from a part of the sentence already begun a few words previously. (New Testament Greek sentences are often very long.)

A Word About Method

Each entry in the following pages is concerned with a single Greek word. These words are given in alphabetical order, in company with their English equivalents. (Two indexes, one Greek and one English, will help you find a particular concept. A Scripture index is also included.)

The first thing you will find under each entry is the citation for a key New Testament passage, followed by the literal Greek, which I will translate for you. The *New American Bible* (NAB) translation of the key passage then appears, and is compared to three other excellent modern translations: the *Jerusalem Bible* (JB), the *New English Bible* (NEB) and the *New International Version* (NIV). Occasionally, where it seems helpful to do so, we will also compare these four translations to the ancient *King James Version* (KJV).

After these comparisons have been made, we will explore as best we can the original Greek sense of the word, and then give examples of how the word under analysis is used in other New Testament passages.

Now let's begin our journey through the Greek New Testament.

Agape—Love

(Ah-gah'-pay)

Key Passage: 1 John 4:16b

Literal Greek: *Ho Theos agape estin, kai ho menon en te*
agape en to Theo menei kai ho Theos en
auto menei. (God is *love* and the one
remaining in *love* remains in God and God
remains in him.)

NAB: God is love,
and he who abides in love
abides in God,
and God in him.

JB: God is love
and anyone who lives in love lives in God,
and God lives in him.

NEB: God is love; he who dwells in love is
dwelling in God, and God in him.

NIV: God is love. Whoever lives in love lives in
God, and God in him.

One could say that the New Testament's core theological
concept is *agape*. That is because, as the key passage shows,
the New Testament seeks essentially to reveal God to its
readers and to show how one may come to share God's life.

In his final prayer before his passion and death Jesus
prays to the Father that *he agape hen egapesas me en autois*
e kago en autois, "the love with which you love me may
be in them and I in them" (Jn 17:26). In other words, Jesus
reveals to humanity the highest love imaginable—the love
which the Father has for the Son—and at the same time
reveals that the Father has this same love for all those he has
created. It is this fact which makes the New Testament
"gospel" or "good news."

Paul constantly taught his readers to live their love responsibly, teaching them that love does not mean freedom to do as one wishes. Rather, genuine love implies putting others' welfare ahead of one's own. In several places in his writings, Paul had to remind his readers that the Christian life, although rooted in love, is rooted in responsible love and not a love of license.

This is shown clearly in Rom 13:8-14, where Paul summarizes the commandments in the familiar Old Testament verse, "Love your neighbor as yourself" (Rom 13:9, quoting Lv 19:18). He then goes on to counsel against various acts of immorality. Perhaps the most famous passage of all of Paul's writings is his eloquent tribute to love in 1 Cor 13. After discussing the various charismatic gifts, Paul shows that the greatest gift is love itself. In 1 Cor 13:2 Paul says if *agapen de me echo* ("I have not love"), then I become little more than *chalkos echon* ("sounding brass") or *kumbalon alalazon* ("tinkling cymbal").

Another word for love, *phileo,* has a slightly different connotation. Whereas *agape* refers to God's very nature, *phileo* refers more to affection, even friendship. One of the most interesting examples of the difference between the two words is Jn 21:15-17.

In 21:15 Jesus asks Peter *agapas me pleon touton,* "Do you love me more than these others?" In 21:16 Jesus once again asks *agapas me,* "Do you love me?" Each time Peter gives an affirmative response: *philo se,* "I love you" (21:16,17). A third time Jesus asks Peter—this time not *agapas me* but rather *phileis me,* "Do you love me?" This question conveys a different sense: "Do you really love me with human affection, Peter? Do you really love me as a brother? Do you simply *like* me?"

By using *phileo* in his third question to Peter, Jesus shows Peter that he forgives his threefold denial on the night of his arrest as one good friend forgives the faults and failings of another. Now all that is forgotten, and Jesus wants Peter to know that he is accepted as friend and brother. Jesus wants Peter to be assured of this before Peter begins his own mission in Jesus' name. John wants all of his readers to know that Jesus has this same tender, human affection he had for Peter for all his disciples, no matter how many times they may deny him.

God's love is thus revealed both in a supernatural sense and a highly human and physical sense. In its supernatural quality, *agape* is God's love as his very nature. All Christians are assured of this love, and will share it eternally. At the same time, God also loves us with tender human affection, as illustrated by the reassurance Jesus gave Peter that all was right between them even after Peter's denial.

Christians often repeat the expected assertion, "God loves me," in the sense of *agape* rather than in the sense of *phileo*. They believe God loves them in the sense of *agape* because this is revealed in Scripture as an essential element of Christian doctrine. But Christians sometimes are more hesitant to believe that God loves them in the sense of *phileo* that God *likes* them.

The New Testament reveals that God *likes* us as well. Do we believe, as the Lord taught Peter, both that we are loved because it is God's nature to love, and also that we are loved (liked) because God chooses to have a tender and affectionate human relationship with us as our dearest and closest friend?

Aleipho—Anoint

(Ah-lay′-foe)

Key Passage: Matthew 6:17

Literal Greek: "...*aleipsai sou ten kephalen kai to proso-pon sou nipsai.*" ("...anoint your head and wash your face.")

NAB: "When you fast, see to it that you groom your hair and wash your face."

JB, NIV: "...put oil on your head and wash your face...."

NEB: "...anoint your head and wash your face...."

Aleipho suggests a more spiritual concept than the NAB's *groom*. For example, in Lk 7:38 the sinful woman *eleiphen* ("anointed") Jesus' feet with ointment. Likewise, when Jesus sent the 12 apostles out on their first mission, they expelled demons and *eleiphon elaio pollous arrostous*, "anointed with oil many sick ones" (Mk 6:13).

Another word for *anoint* used in the Greek New Testament is *chrio*, which takes on more of a sacramental meaning. For example, in Luke's Gospel, Jesus quotes Isaiah's words: "...wherefore he *echrisen* (anointed) me to evangelize the poor" (Lk 4:18). In Acts 4:27 Jesus is referred to as the one whom God *echrisas* ("did anoint").

The title *Christ* (*Christos*) is derived from this same verb. In 2 Cor 1:21 Paul plays on the   ds *Christ* and *anointed* so as to associate Christians with Christ through their anointing; he says that God *chrisas* ("having anointed us") has made Christians one *Christon* ("in Christ").

Paul's use of this verb testifies to the New Testament's understanding of anointing as an action by which God sanctifies his people and separates them from the world—the sacramental means by which Christians receive the gift of the

Holy Spirit. In this respect see 1 Jn 2:20, where the writer refers to Christians as having *chrisma* ("anointing") *apo tou hagiou kai oidate pantes*, "from the Holy One you all know" and thus receive the gift of wisdom.

Anastasis—Resurrection

(Ahn-ah'-stah-sis)

Key Passage:	John 11:25
Literal Greek:	"...*ego eimi he anastasis kai he zoe.*" ("I am the *resurrection* and the life.")
NAB:	"I am the resurrection and the life ..."
JB:	"I am the resurrection."*
NEB:	"I am the resurrection and I am life."
NIV:	"I am the resurrection and the life."

Anastasis is derived from *histemi* ("to cause to stand") and *ana* ("up"), therefore, "causing to stand up." In Luke's Gospel the words of the holy elder Simeon are indeed prophetic when he tells Mary that her young son will be the cause of the *unastasin pollon*, "the rising again of many" (Lk 2:34). As the key passage shows, Jesus would appropriate these very words when he raised Lazarus from the dead by saying that he (Jesus) is the *anastasis* (Jn 11:25).

Luke refers to the *anastasei ton dikaion*, "the resurrection of the just" (Lk 14:14), meaning that the elect will follow Jesus to a resurrected life of glory. We must distinguish, however, between *anastasis* and the resuscitation of Lazarus which Jesus brought about in Jn 11:43-44. The author does not say that Lazarus was resurrected, but simply that he

---

* Several ancient manuscripts omit the words *kai he zoe*.

13

exelthen, "came out" (11:44). Lazarus would die again and *then* experience Jesus' promised resurrection of the just. *Anastasis* does not mean a return to one's past form of existence, but going ahead into a radically new form.

Antichristos—Antichrist

(Ahn-teé-chris-taws)

Key Passage: 1 John 2:22

Literal Greek: ...*outos estin ho antichristos, ho arnoumenos ton patera kai ton huion.* (This is the *antichrist*, the one denying the father and the son.)

NAB: He is the antichrist,
denying the Father and the Son.

JB: He is Antichrist;
and he is denying the Father as well as the Son....

NEB: He is Antichrist, for he denies both the Father and the Son.

NIV: Such a man is the antichrist—he denies the Father and the Son.

The word *antichrist* is found only in John's Epistles, but the figure appears to be suggested by the "man of lawlessness" (NAB: "son of perdition") in 2 Thes 2:3. The antichrist is someone who opposes Christ, and is to be distinguished from the *pseudochristoi* ("false Christs" or "false messiahs") of Mt 24:24 who will give great signs and marvels in order to cause Christians to err. Mark also refers to *pseudochristoi* and *pseudoprophetai* ("false prophets") who will *apoplanan* ("lead astray") the chosen ones (Mk 13:22).

14

Aphiemi—Forgive

(Ah-fie-ay-mee)

Key Passage: Matthew 6:14

Literal Greek: "...*Ean gar aphete tois anthropois ta paraptomata auton, aphesei kai humin ho pater humon ho ouranios.*" ("For if you *forgive* men their trespasses your heavenly Father will also *forgive* you.")

NAB: "If you forgive the faults of others, your heavenly Father will forgive you yours."

JB: "Yes, if you forgive others their failings, your heavenly Father will forgive you yours...."

NEB: "For if you forgive others the wrongs they have done, your heavenly Father will also forgive you...."

NIV: "For if you forgive men when they sin against you, your heavenly Father will also forgive you."

Aphiemi is derived from the verb *hiemi* ("to send") and *apo* ("from"). The word thus literally means "to send from," and underscores the fact that what is sent away or forgiven is no longer present.

This is made clear in Matthew's parable of the unforgiving servant (18:21-35). In 18:27 the master *splagchnistheis* ("filled with tenderness") *apelusen* ("forgave" or, more technically, "cancelled") the loan which he had given to his servant. It is in this sense of the total cancellation of debts that the New Testament uses *forgive*. In Mt 9:2, therefore, Jesus exhorts the paralytic to be of good cheer because *aphientai sou hai hamartiai*, "your sins are forgiven you."

This connotation is taken over into the related noun *aphesis*, "forgiveness" or "release," the latter word being the

15

more accurate translation. In Eph 1:7 the author states that in Jesus Christ we have *aphesin ton paraptomaton*, "the release of trespasses"—perhaps a better rendering of the Greek than the NAB's "sins forgiven." The sense of the passage is that the debt is now completely cancelled.

The New Testament teaches a positive dimension to forgiveness: rehabilitation or complete restoration of liberty and freedom. This understanding is frequently lacking in our use of "forgiveness of sin." Christians are not only forgiven, they are set free for a new life.

Apokalupsis—Revelation

(Ah-pawk-ah'-loop-sis)

Key Passage: Revelation 1:1

Literal Greek: *Apokalupsis Iesou Christou, hen edoken auto ho Theos....(A revelation of Jesus Christ, which God gave to him....)*

NAB: This is the revelation God gave to Jesus Christ, that he might show his servants what must happen very soon.

JB: This is the revelation given by God to Jesus Christ so that he could tell his servants about the things which are now to take place very soon....

NEB: This is the revelation given by God to Jesus Christ. It was given to him so that he might show his servants what must shortly happen.

NIV: The revelation of Jesus Christ, which God gave him to show his servants what must soon take place.

Apokalupsis is related to the verb *apokalupto* which connotes "to take the cover away from something, to reveal." As the key passage shows, one of its principal uses in the New Testament is to refer to the transmission of God's Word to humanity. *Apokalupsis* thus refers to God's plan to save humanity, as in Rom 16:25, where Paul refers to his own role in revealing God's plan as *apokalupsin musteriou,* "revelation of the mystery."

Apokalupsis is also used to speak of Christ's Second Coming, as where Paul writes about his readers' eager expectation for *ten apokalupsin tou kuriou,* "the revelation of the Lord" (1 Cor 1:7). The author of 2 Thes expresses this same thought when he writes about Jesus' Second Coming as the *apokalupsei...ap ouranou met aggelon dunameos,* "the revelation from heaven with angels of power" (1:7).

When Jesus does come again in glory, not only will *he* be revealed, but also the "sons of God." Paul says that, just as Christians eagerly await the revelation of Christ at the end of time, so too *tes ktiseos* ("the creation") awaits *ten apokalupsin ton huion tou Theou,* "the revelation of the sons of God" (Rom 8:19).

Apolutrosis—Redemption

(Ah-paw-loo'-tro-sis)

Key Passage: Romans 3:24

Literal Greek: *...dikaioumenoi dorean te autou chariti dia*
                 tes apolutroseos tes en Christo Iesou....
                 (...being justified freely by the grace of
                 him through the *redemption* in Christ Jesus.)

NAB: All men are now undeservedly justified by
         the gift of God, through the redemption
         wrought in Christ Jesus.

JB: ...justified through the free gift of his grace
         by being redeemed in Christ Jesus....

NEB: ...and all are justified by God's free grace
         alone, through his act of liberation in the
         person of Christ Jesus.

NIV: ...and are justified freely by his grace
         through the redemption that came by Christ
         Jesus.

Apolutrosis comes from *lutrosis* ("deliverance") and *lutroo*, meaning to release a captive or prisoner upon receiving a ransom. *Apolutrosis* thus connotes deliverance from imprisonment by one who has paid a ransom for the captive's release.

Luke uses *apolutrosis* to describe the effect upon the elect of Jesus' Second Coming when he records Jesus' words to his disciples: "When these things begin to happen, stand erect and hold your heads high, for your *apolutrosis* [translated 'deliverance' in the NAB] is near at hand" (Lk 21:28).

As the key passage shows, *apolutrosis* is also used to signify the present result of Jesus' death on the cross for those who believe in him. This thought is found in Eph 1:7,

18

where the author says of Christ that he is the one *en ho echomen ten apolutrosin dia tou haimatos autou*, "in whom we have the redemption through his blood." The author places this clause in apposition to a clause which reads *ten aphesin ton paraptomaton*, "the forgiveness of trespasses," showing that our redemption is first and foremost a deliverance from sin and its effects.

To emphasize that Christ is the ongoing source of deliverance for all people, Paul refers to Christ not as our "redeemer," but as our *apolutrosis*, our "redemption" (1 Cor 1:30). Christ's act of redemption in creation is not finished. It continues even until the end of time, delivering every aspect of creation from the power of sin and death.

Apostolos   Apostle

(Ah paws' taw-loss)

Key Passage: Hebrews 3:1

Literal Greek: *...katanoesate ton apostolon kai archierea tes homologias hemon Iesoun....* (...consider Jesus, the *apostle* and high priest of our confession....)

NAB: ...fix your eyes on Jesus, the apostle and high priest whom we acknowledge in faith....

JB: ...turn your minds to Jesus, the apostle and the high priest of our religion.

NEB: ...think of the Apostle and High Priest of the religion we profess....

NIV: ...fix your thoughts on Jesus, the apostle and high priest whom we confess.

19

The word *apostolos* is a combination of *apo* and *stello*, "forth" and "send," respectively. *Apostolos* thus means "one who is sent forth." As Heb 3:1 indicates, the apostle *par excellence* is Jesus himself.

Apostolos connotes a commissioning, giving someone one's own authority to take up or continue a mission already begun. Heb 3:1 emphasizes this concept of Jesus as the commissioned representative of the Father, the one who continues and fulfills the Father's work of forming a people and saving humanity. John's Gospel refers to Jesus in this same sense when it calls Jesus *hon apesteilas*, "he whom God sent" (17:3).

During the exercise of his own apostolic mission, Jesus likewise commissioned apostles to carry on his mission after his death. In Luke's version of the commissioning of the apostles (6:13), Jesus "called to him the disciples, and choosing from them twelve, *hous kai apostolous onomasen*," that is, "he *also* named them apostles." In other words, Jesus raised the status of 12 of his disciples to a new level by sharing with them the very apostolic authority given to him by his Father.

In the early Church other elders were referred to as apostles, and thus the word came to take on a more expanded meaning. Paul referred to himself as an apostle in 1 Cor 9:1—*ouk eimi apostolos?* ("Am I not an apostle?"). In Acts 14:14 Barnabas is referred to as an apostle; the word is also used of Andronicus and Junias, who are said to be *episemoi en tois apostolois*, "notable among the apostles" (Rom 16:7).

Thus we see that the definition of *apostle* extends in certain cases beyond the Twelve themselves. In a sense, every Christian is an apostle in that he or she is commissioned by Jesus to carry on the mission which he engaged in on earth. The Church has long upheld this secondary understanding of *apostolos*—in its concept of the "lay apostolate," for instance.

The concept of apostolic authority as we understand it today is represented both in the word *apostolos* and in other words such as *histemi* ("appoint") and *kathistemi* ("appoint

to a place of authority"). For example, in Acts 6:3 the
apostles select seven assistants, *hous katastesomen* ("whom
we will appoint"). In Acts 14:23, Paul and Barnabas
cheirotonesantes...presbuterous ("having appointed elders")
"committed them to the Lord in whom they had believed."
The verb *cheirotoneo*, a combination of *teino* ("to stretch")
and *cheir* ("hand") is closely akin to our concept of
ordination.

Artos—Bread

(ahr'-toss)

Key Passage: Matthew 6:11

Literal Greek: *"Ton arton hemon ton epiousion dos hemin
                 semeron."* ("The daily *bread* of us give to us
                 today.")

NAB: "Give us today our daily bread...."

JB,NEB,NIV: Identical to NAB.

Bread, in Jesus' time, connoted a small, thin loaf made of
flour and water. Such loaves were not cut, but broken
or torn before being eaten. Some of the newly baked loaves
were consecrated to the Lord as "holy bread" (Mt 12:4),
literally, *artous tes protheseos*, "loaves of the setting forth"
(JB: "loaves of offering"; NEB: "sacred bread"; NIV: "consecrated bread").

Jesus took *arton* ("a loaf") at the Last Supper (Mt 26:26)
and *eklasen*—"broke"—it before he distributed portions of it
to his disciples, telling them that it was *soma mou*, "my
body." Thenceforth, the Eucharist was colloquially referred to
in the early Church as *klasei tou artou*, the "breaking of
the bread" (Acts 2:42). Paul wrote that *ton arton hon
klomen*—"the bread which we break"—is *koinonia tou*

21

somatos tou Christou, "a communion of the body of Christ" (1 Cor 10:16).

In John's Gospel (6:35), Jesus says *ego eimi ho artos tes zoes,* "I am the bread of life." In the same discourse (6:55), Jesus emphasizes that his flesh *(sarx)* is *alethes brosis,* "true food," and that his blood *(haima)* is *alethes posis* or "true drink." The Greek mandates against a purely metaphorical or symbolic interpretation of Jesus' words. Jesus is telling people that they must somehow literally eat his body.

The verb which John uses for "eating" is *trogon* ("the one *eating* of me," 6:56, and "the one *eating* me," 6:58). *Trogon* connotes eating audibly, so that perhaps our words *munch* or *crunch* would be a modern equivalent. In the Greek there is no trace of a suggestion that Jesus sees himself as bread in simply an allegorical sense.

Baptisma—Baptism

(Bahp'-tis-mah)

Key Passage: Matthew 28:19

Literal Greek: "...*baptizontes autous eis to onoma tou patros kai tou huiou kai tou hagiou pneumatos.*" ("...*baptizing* them in the name of the Father and of the Son and of the Holy Spirit.")

NAB: "...go, therefore, and make disciples of all the nations. Baptize them in the name 'of the Father, and of the Son and of the Holy Spirit.'"

JB,NEB,NIV: Virtually identical to NAB.

The Greek word *baptisma* is derived from *bapto,* which means "dip." See, for example, Lk 16:24, where the rich man begs Abraham to send Lazarus to him *hina bapse to akron tou daktulou,* "that he may *dip* the tip of the finger...." In Jn 13:26 Jesus says, *ego bapso to psomion,* "I shall *dip* the morsel." The noun *baptisma* thus connotes the process of dipping or submerging.

The evangelists took the word and applied it to the rite which John the Baptist used prior to Jesus' public mission. John preached a baptism of repentance, a baptism different from that contemplated in the key passage above.

Christian Baptism not only removes sin, but also identifies the Christian with the death, burial and resurrection of the Lord. Paul makes this clear in Rom 6, where he reminds us that *ebaptisthemen,* "we were baptized" into Christ (6:3). And through our *baptismatos* "into his death, we are raised with Christ from the dead" (6:4).

The word has additional connotations, as in Lk 12:50, where Jesus refers to his coming passion and death as *baptisma,* and Mk 10:38-39, where Jesus asks his disciples if they can be "baptized" with his *baptisma,* meaning his sufferings.

In Acts 19:1-7, Luke makes it clear that Christian Baptism confers the gifts of the Holy Spirit. In this passage Paul encounters people who have received John's baptism but who have not heard of the Holy Spirit. Accordingly, Paul baptizes the people *eis to onoma tou kuriou Iesou,* "in the name of the Lord Jesus" (19:5). After receiving this Baptism and after Paul lays hands on them, they begin to manifest the gifts of the Holy Spirit. Accordingly, Paul's actions are usually referred to as "the baptism of the Holy Spirit," although the passage itself does not contain these words.

Basileia—Kingdom

(Bahs-eel-ay'-ah)

Key Passage: Matthew 25:34b

Literal Greek: *"...kleronomesate ten hetoimasmenen humin basileian apo kataboles kosmou."* ("Inherit the *kingdom* having been prepared for you from the foundation of the world.")

NAB: "Inherit the kingdom prepared for you from the creation of the world."

JB: "...take for your heritage the kingdom prepared for you since the foundation of the world."

NEB: "...come, enter and possess the kingdom that has been ready for you since the world was made."

NIV: "...take your inheritance, the kingdom prepared for you since the creation of the world."

Basileia primarily connotes sovereignty or kingly authority. In the New Testament it frequently has the secondary meaning of a geographical *region* ruled by a king, as in Mt 4:8, where the devil shows Jesus *tas basileias tou kosmou*, "the kingdoms of the world."

The primary connotation of *basileia* is seen in 1 Cor 15:24, where Paul speaks of Jesus reigning until he delivers the *basileian* to God, after having abolished *pasan archen kai pasan exousian kai dunamin*, "all rule and all authority and power." In other words, the fulfillment of Jesus' Kingdom is at the same time the full manifestation of his power, authority and rule over all creation.

The kingdom is a *musterion* (mystery) since it *is* present but has *not yet* been manifested. Jesus tells the Pharisees that the *basilei* is not a matter of *paratereseos*, "observation"

24

(Lk 17:20); that is, the Kingdom is not always seen or recognized. And as we saw in the key passage, the Kingdom will not be manifest in its full glory until the final judgment.

The here-and-now aspect of the Kingdom is recognized through the Christian's everyday suffering; in 2 Thes 1:4-5, the writer says that suffering is evidence of God's judgment that the believer is worthy *tes basileias*, "of the kingdom." In Acts 14:22 Paul and Barnabas encourage the disciples to suffer hardship patiently so that (in the future) they will *eiselthein eis te basileian*, "enter into the kingdom."

In Lk 17:21 Jesus says that the *basileia* is *entos humon*, "within you," in the sense that it is in your midst. What Luke means here is that God's sovereignty and authority is fully present in Jesus' person. To enter into Jesus' Kingdom one must first accept Jesus' authority and rule in one's life. In the New Testament Jesus and his Kingdom are thus one, in the sense that a king and his authority cannot be separated. Further, it is not human ability or power which enables a person to enter into the Kingdom. Rather, one must be *gennethe ex hudatos kai pneumatos*, "born of water and Spirit," before one can enter into the *basileian tou Theou* (Jn 3:5).

Matthew, instead of "kingdom of God," prefers *basileian ton ouranon*, "kingdom of the heavens" (e.g., Mt 7:21).* This kingdom of the heavens is equivalent to Mt's and Lk's "kingdom of God," or Mt's own *basileia tou patros mou*, "kingdom of my Father" (Mt 26:29).

Christians are reminded to pray for the future realization of the Kingdom in the prayer which Jesus taught his disciples: *elthato he basilei sou*, "let come your kingdom"

---

* Readers of the NAB will notice that Mt 7:21 reads "kingdom of God" instead of the literal "kingdom of the heavens," perhaps to avoid redundancy; the Greek ends ". . .the will of my Father in the heavens." The NAB sometimes alternates between "*kingdom* of God" (as in Mt 7:21; 19:24) and "*reign* of God" (as in Mt 13:24). The distinction appears to be based on the context. For example, in Mt 7:21 and 19:24 the word *kingdom* makes more sense in English after the verb *enter*, while the word *reign* better expresses the all-encompassing nature of *basileia* in the parables of Mt 13.

25

(Mt 6:10). The early Christians ardently looked forward to the day of Jesus' *parousia*, "coming," as the full realization of God's power (see p. 107).

(see p. 107)

Diakonos—Deacon, Servant

(Dee-ah'-kon-aws)

Key Passage: Matthew 20:26

Literal Greek: *"...Hos ean thele en humin megas genesthai, estai humon diakonos...."* ("Whoever wishes among you to become great will be your *servant.*")

NAB: "Anyone among you who aspires to greatness must serve the rest...."

JB,NEB,NIV: Virtually identical to NAB.

Diakonos is likely derived from *dioko*, which can mean "to run after or pursue," in the sense of striving for or seeking after. For example, *dioko* is used in Phil 3:14, where Paul says *dioko eis to brabeion,* "I pursue [or seek after] the prize...."

In the New Testament the chief *diakonos* (servant) is Christ himself. In Rom 15:8 Paul says that Christ has become *diakonon,* or "the servant of the Jews because of God's faithfulness...." Those who follow Jesus must also be servants: *"kai hopou eimi ego, ekei kai ho diakonos ho emos estai,"* "and where I am there also my servant will be" (Jn 12:26). In this respect, note that women are considered equal servants with men; Paul commends Phoebe as *diakonon tes ekklesias,* "a servant of the Church" (Rom 16:1).

Diakonos is to be distinguished from *doulos,* which can also mean "servant," but more specifically denotes a slave. The distinction between the two is illustrated in Mt 22:2-14.

26

The king in this parable sends out *tous doulous,* "the slaves," to call the guests to the wedding feast (22:2, 4, 6, 8, 10). At the end of the parable, however, when the king ejects the man who does not have the wedding garment, he uses not his *duloi* but his *diakonois* (22:13). *Doulos* is one in an indentured position, while *diakonos* reflects a more exalted relationship and is reserved for one who has the authority to act for the master and on his behalf.

Related words are *leitourgos* and *huperetes.* The former is usually translated "minister." For example, Heb 8:2 calls Christ *leitourgos,* "minister," of the sanctuary. Paul refers to himself as *leitourgon Christou Iesou eis ta ethne,* "a minister of Christ Jesus to the nations" (Rom 15:16).

Huperetes is an interesting word, a combination of *hupo* ("under") and *eretes* ("a rower"), thus suggesting someone who rows under the authority of another. The image suggested is that of rowers of a racing shell under the direction of a coxswain. In Lk 4:20, after reading from the scroll of Isaiah, Jesus returns the scroll to the *huperete* and sits down. In the NAB and the JB, this word is translated as "assistant," "attendant" in the NEB and the NIV. The KJV has "minister," a valid translation of the term which is perhaps incorrect in this context.

In Acts 26:16 Paul, recounting his vision on the road to Damascus, quotes Jesus as saying Paul has been appointed as *hupereten kui martura* ("attendant and witness"). *Martura* means "witness," and here the NAB translates *hupereten* as "servant" (as do the JB, NEB and NIV).

Thus the New Testament uses several terms for *servant;* we should distinguish the meaning of the various terms by focusing on their context.

Diatheke—Covenant

(Dee-ah-thay'-kay)

Key Passage: Matthew 26:28

Literal Greek: "...*touto gar estin to haima mou tes diathekes....*" ("...for this is my blood of the *covenant....*")

NAB: "...for this is my blood, the blood of the covenant, to be poured out in behalf of many for the forgiveness of sins."

JB,NEB,NIV: Virtually identical to NAB.

The Church, of course, did not invent the concept of covenant. It was taken over from the Jews, for whom it expressed the central feature of their relationship with Yahweh. Technically, *diatheke* means a bequest of property made in a will (a "testament"). The Hebrew word was *berith*, which connotes "divide"—interestingly, the opposite of our modern conception of covenant as a coming together.

The covenant made Israel different from all other peoples; no other people had the same kind of relationship with God. Through the covenant God planned to save his people and to establish a relationship with them. Two essential elements of the Old Testament covenant were a sacred meal (Ex 24:9-11) and a washing in blood (Ex 24:4-8), suggesting intimate communion with God in a sacramental way.

The concept of dividing is carried over from the Hebrew *berith* into the Greek *diatheke*. Also contained in the New Testament understanding of *covenant* are the same key elements: a sacramental meal and a washing in blood. At the Last Supper Jesus refers to his coming death as a *diatheke*. At the sacred meal of the new covenant (the new testament), Jesus prepares to die for the sins of humanity, washing them in his blood and thus freeing them from sin.

The early Church emphasized that through Jesus' death

28

Christians were heirs of the covenant. In Acts 3:25 Peter says, "You are the heirs of the *diathekes* [covenant] God made with your fathers...." The author of Hebrews refers to Christ as *diathekes kaines mesites*, "mediator of a new covenant" (Heb 9:15). Notice that the same word, *diatheke*, is used in Heb 9:16-17, but in the context of these verses the word is more properly rendered "testament" as in the NAB, or "will" as in the JB.

There is no contradiction between the two senses of *covenant* used here, since Jesus bequeaths new life for those who believe in him. Further, a will is a means by which a person divides property and gives it to others. Thus *diatheke*, whether understood as "covenant" (as in Mt 26:28) or as "will" (as in Heb 9:16-17) fully expresses the concept that Jesus brings to humanity the gift of new life.

Didache—Teaching, Doctrine

(Did-ah-kay')

Key Passage: Matthew 7:28

Literal Greek: *Kai egeneto hote etelesen ho Iesous logous toutous, exeplessonto hoi ochloi epi te didache autou.* (And it came to pass when Jesus finished these words the crowds were astounded at his *teaching*.)

NAB: Jesus finished this discourse and left the crowds spellbound at his teaching.

JB: Jesus had now finished what he wanted to say, and his teaching made a deep impression on the people....

NEB: When Jesus had finished this discourse the people were astounded at his teaching....

NIV: When Jesus had finished saying these things, the crowds were amazed at his teaching....

Didache is derived from *didasko*, "to teach." It can refer to the subject matter of something taught, as in our key passage. *Didache* can also refer to the act of teaching itself, as in Mk 4:2. There the evangelist refers to Jesus' speaking in parables as *didache autou*, "his teaching," in the sense of his *act* of telling the crowd a parable.

There are several related words in the New Testament. *Didaskalos* means "teacher," as in Lk 2:46 where the boy Jesus is sitting in the Temple amid *ton didaskalon*, "the teachers" of the Law. A more precise word for teacher of the Law is *nomodidaskalos* (the Greek word for "law" is *nomos*). We find a reference to these *nomodidaskaloi* in Acts 5:34, where the word is used of Gamaliel, the famous rabbi under whom Paul studied.

Another word for "teaching" is *didaskalia*, as in Eph 4:14, where the writer cautions against listening to every *anemo tes didaskalias,* "wind of teaching." For some reason, *didaskalia* becomes more common usage than *didache* in the later writings of the New Testament. For example, *didache* is used twice in the Pastoral Letters (1 and 2 Tm, Ti), whereas *didaskalia* occurs some 15 times in these late New Testament works. In the Gospels, which were written earlier, only *didache* occurs, except in two instances (Mt 15:9 and Mk 7:7) where *didaskalia* is used to translate an Old Testament quotation.

It is interesting that two of the early Church's most important writings were the *Diduche* and the *Didaskalia,* manuals of Christian doctrine which originated in the East— perhaps from the Syrian Church—in the second and third centuries, respectively.

Dikaiosune—
Righteousness, Justice

(Dick-eye-ah-soon´-ay)

Key Passage: Romans 6:18

Literal Greek: *...eleutherothentes de apo tes hamartias edoulothete te dikaiosune.* (...and having been freed from sin you were enslaved to *righteousness.*)

NAB: ...freed from your sin, you became slaves of justice.

JB: You may have been freed from the slavery of sin, but only to become "slaves" of righteousness.

NEB: ...emancipated from sin, [you] have become slaves of righteousness....

NIV: You have been set free from sin and have become slaves to righteousness.

There is perhaps no more significant term in all of Paul's letters than *dikaiousune.* As we shall see, it is related to several other words which are likewise highly significant to Paul's theology. *Dikaiosune* translates most correctly as the NAB's "justice."

The term was one of the principal theological concepts by which Paul taught the significance of Jesus' death and resurrection. By "justice" Paul is suggesting the idea of "right-standing." For Paul only God is just or upright, and humanity can achieve this state of uprightness (*dikaiosune*) only through God's salvation. *Dikaiosune* becomes for Paul the term which more than any other signifies the right relationship with God achieved for humanity by Jesus. Paul stresses that such a state of righteousness or justice cannot be attained by observance of the Law, but comes

32

only through faith in Christ.

The related verb is *dikaioo*, meaning "to make just" or "to make right." In Rom 5:1 Paul makes it clear that *dikaiothentes* ("having been justified") *ek pisteos* ("by faith"), we now have *prosagogen*, "access" to God's grace. Paul's righteousness comes from faith, not from the Law.

James likewise used the verb *dikaioo* in his writing. He says that humanity *dikaioutai* ("is justified") *ouk ek pisteos monon*, "not by faith alone" (James 2:24). James wanted to stress that faith is not simply an act of *belief*, but an act of *commitment* to one's brothers and sisters shown by deeds of loving service.

The related adjective is *dikaios* ("just"). In Jn 17:25 Jesus addresses his father as *Pater dikaie*, "righteous" or "just Father." Luke describes Zechariah and Elizabeth as *dikaioi* (Lk 1:6). In Jn 5:30 Jesus refers to his judgment as *dikaia*.

Doron—Gift

(Doe'-rawn)

Key Passage: Ephesians 2:8

Literal Greek: . . . *kai touto ouk ex humon, Theou to doron.* (. . . and this [salvation] is not of you, it is the *gift* of God.)

NAB: This is not your own doing, it is God's gift.

JB: . . . not by anything of your own, but by a gift from God. . . .

NEB: . . . it is not your own doing. It is God's gift. . . .

NIV: . . . and this not from yourselves, it is the gift of God. . . .

There are several Greek words with different connotations for *gift*. *Doron* as used in the key passage describes the free, unmerited gift of salvation by faith. *Doron* also has the ordinary connotation of a gift made to the poor (as in Lk 21:1, where Jesus watches people putting their *dora* into the Temple treasury).

A related word is *dorea*, as in Jn 4:10, where Jesus tells the Samaritan woman, "If you only knew *ten dorean tou Theou* (the gift of God). . . ." Paul uses the same word in 2 Cor 9:15: "Thanks be to God for his indescribable *dorea* (gift)!" Unlike *doron*, *dorea* is used only in a spiritual sense, referring to the gift of God's grace or salvation. *Dorea* is never used in the New Testament to refer to a present or donation from one human being to another.

A related word is *charisma*, which likewise means "gift," and likewise connotes the unmerited favor which God shows to humanity, his self-revelation and self-gift. In one place, Paul uses *charisma* and *dorea* in the same verse: "But the gift (*charisma*) is not like the offense. For if by the offense of the one man all died, much more did the grace of God and the gracious gift (*dorea*) of the one man, Jesus Christ, abound for all" (Rom 5:15).

Here the difference between *charisma* and *dorea* is revealed: *Charisma* has no modifier, but means in itself "free gift," while *dorea* has the modifier *en chariti*, "in grace." In other words, Paul added the explanation (translated "gracious" in the NAB) to the word *dorea to* emphasize the free character of Jesus' gift, while taking it for granted that his readers understood that *charisma* connotes gratuitousness.

Perhaps Paul's most famous use of *charisma* is in his teaching on the spiritual gifts in 1 Cor 12—13. In 1 Cor 12:4 he says, *Diaireseis de charismaton eisin to de auto pneuma* ("Now differences of gifts there are, but the same Spirit"). Paul goes on to name the various gifts and to describe their purpose in the Body of Christ.

Charism's connotation reflects *charis*, "grace." For Paul gift is grace, and grace is gift. Luke writes of this grace in his description of the maturing child Jesus: *charis Theou en ep auto*, "the grace of God was upon him" (Lk 2:40).

34

This same *charis* resided in the early Church and was given to the first evangelists, as Luke points out in Acts 14:26: Paul and Barnabas had *te chariti tou Theou eis to ergon ho eplerosan*, "the grace of God for the work which they accomplished."

This *charis* comes from God the Father (*chariti Theou*, see 2 Cor 1:12), and also from Jesus. In Gal 1:6 Paul reminds his readers that they are called *en chariti Christou*, "by the grace of Christ." Grace is a gift only of God; Jesus has the prerogative to bestow grace because of his own divine nature.

Charis is in contrast to *ergon* ("works"), as in Rom 11:6 where Paul contrasts his new gospel of grace to the Jewish reliance on works of the Law. In Rom 6:14 Paul reminds his readers *ou gar este hupo nomon alla hupo charin*, "for you are not under law but under grace."

Another interesting New Testament word for *gift* is *merismos*, which literally means a division into parts. The NAB translates Heb 2:4b as ". . . and distribution of the gifts of the Holy Spirit as he willed." The Greek reads *kai pneumatos hagiou merismois kata ten autou thelesin*; literally, "and by distributions according to the Spirit's will." Like the other words for gift we have considered, *merismos* likewise clearly stresses the sense that God freely shares himself with humanity.

Dunamis—Might, Power

(Doon'-ah-miss)

Key Passage: Acts 1:8

Literal Greek: *"Alla lempsesthe dunamin epelthontos tou hagiou pneumatos eph humas...."* ("But you will receive *power* with the coming upon you of the Holy Spirit.")

NAB: "You will receive power when the Holy Spirit comes down on you...."

JB,NEB,NIV: Virtually identical to NAB.

The essential contrast between the life of Jesus' disciples *before* his death and resurrection, and their life *after* is that in the first instance they were weak and powerless. After they received the Holy Spirit, however, they were filled with an unprecedented power to do the very works which Jesus himself did. A Christianity which does not enable humanity to have this power for new life is a Christianity stripped of one of its essential elements.

After Pentecost Peter, the very disciple who, because of his lack of courage, had disowned Jesus, becomes one of the most powerful witnesses to Jesus' Resurrection. In Acts 3:12, shortly after he has healed a cripple in Jesus' name, Peter tells the onlookers who have witnessed the miracle that they erroneously attribute the miracle to *idia dunamei,* "our own power." Peter wants them to understand that they should instead attribute the miracle to the power of God.

Interestingly, Peter had earlier told the Jews that God had testified to Jesus' lordship through the *dunamesi,* "powerful deeds" (Acts 2:22) which Jesus had performed. The same word is used of the "great miracles" (Acts 8:13, NAB) which Philip performed once he himself had received the power of the Holy Spirit. Thus, the same word is used in the New Testament for the *power* which the disciples received from the Holy Spirit as well as for the *deeds* which they performed as a result of receiving this power.

As a result, our word *miracle* is often in the New Testament simply a variation of the word *dunamis,* such as in 1 Cor 12:10 where Paul refers to a charismatic gift known as *energemata dunameon,* or as the NAB has it, "miraculous powers" (1 Cor 12:10). Another word for miracle is *semeion,* "sign," a more typical word for *miracle* in the four Gospels.

Eikon—Image

(Eye-cone')

Key Passage: Colossians 1:15

Literal Greek: ...*hos estin eikon tou Thoou tou aoratou,,,* (...who is an *image* of the invisible God.)

NAB: He is the image of the invisible God....

JB: He is the image of the unseen God....

NEB, NIV: Identical to NAB.

The New Testament uses *eikon* in several ways. For example, in Rom 1:23 Paul uses the word *eikonos* to refer to the images which the pagans used in worshiping false gods. In this sense *eikon* would be a likeness or representation of something else.

Yet, in Heb 10:1 the author uses the word to suggest the *reality of* something. He says that the law was only an *ekian* ("shadow") of the good things to come and not the *eikona* ("image") of these things.

The principal theological significance of *eikon* concerns the relationship between the Father and Christ, and the relationship between Christ and humanity. Our key passage illustrates how *eikon* is used to connote Christ as the Father's image. In 1 Cor 11:7 Paul uses the word to show that man is likewise the *eikon kai doxa Theou,* "the image and glory of God." Humanity as God's image is variously translated as "the new self" (NIV) or "a new man" (NAB).

Humanity's likeness to God (its Godly image) is still being made manifest; there is work yet to be done before humanity becomes a perfect representation of God. This is brought out in 1 Cor 15:49: "As we bore the image of the earthly man, [we shall bear] *ten eikona*, the image of the heavenly man." Humanity's likeness to God is at present a spiritual reality growing evermore towards visible manifestation.

The author of Hebrews uses another word to refer to Christ's likeness to the Father. This word is *charakter*, from which we get our English word *character*. In Heb 1:3 the author says that Christ is the *charakter tes hupostaseos autou* ("the character of the Father's reality"). The NAB translates *charakter* as "exact representation"; the NEB as "stamp," the JB as "the perfect copy" and the NIV as "the exact representation." Each of these translations is groping for a way to express a distinction between *eikon* and *charakter*.

The latter connotes the absolute fullness of relationship between two things or persons compared. It can mean a stamp used to make an image, similar to the notary public seal which makes an impression on a piece of paper. The NEB follows this connotation of *charakter*, while the three other versions emphasize complete likeness between Christ and the Father.

Ekklesia—Assembly

(Ay-klay-seé-ah)

Key Passage: Matthew 16:18

Literal Greek: ". . . oikodomeso mou ten ekklesian." ("I will build of me the church.")

NAB: ". . . on this rock I will build my church. . . ."

JB,NEB,NIV: Virtually identical to NAB.

Ekklesia is a combination of kaleo ("to call") and ek ("out of"). Thus, an ekklesia is a "calling out of" or a "calling forth from."

In Acts 19:39 the city official of Ephesus quells a possible riot by reminding his fellow citizens that they must settle the dispute in the ennomo ekklesia, "lawful assembly." Interestingly, just a few verses earlier the mob referred to itself as ekklesia. In his speech to the Jews in Acts 7:38 Stephen refers to the ancient Israelites in the desert as ekklesia.

In Mt 16:18 Jesus appropriates the word to the body of people he calls forth and forms. The early Church adapted ekklesia to its own use. The writer of Ephesians refers to Jesus as being head over all things te ekklesia, "for the Church," and in Eph 5:23 the writer says that Christ is head tes ekklesias, "of the Church."

Paul uses the word to refer to local congregations. 1 Thes begins te ekklesia Thessalonikeon, "to the Church of the Thessalonians." By the last decade of the first century, Christian writers had so standardized the use of ekklesia for "church" that the writer of 1 Tm 3:5 can ask how anyone who cannot manage his own family can take care of ekklesias Theou, "a church of God."

Eklektos—
Chosen One, the Elect

(Eck-leck-toss')

Key Passage: Romans 8:33

Literal Greek: ...*tis egkalesei kata eklekton Theou?* (Who will bring a charge against the *chosen ones* of God?)

NAB: Who shall bring a charge against God's chosen ones?

JB: Could anyone accuse those that God has chosen?

NEB: Who will be the accuser of God's chosen ones?

NIV: Who will bring any charge against those whom God has chosen?

Eklektos is derived from *lego* ("to pick out") and *ek* ("from"). The principal "chosen one" is Jesus himself; in Lk 23:35 Jesus' tormentors mock him as *ho eklektos*. Mt, Mk and Lk use the word in passages referring to the Last Judgment (Mt 24:22, 24, 31; Mk 13:20, 22, 27). Luke's version (18:7) is a parable about the unjust judge who is beside himself because of the widow's constant pleading. The point of the parable is that God will bring justice to his *eklekton* ("chosen ones," 18:7) who plead with him day and night.

The concept of election or being chosen depends completely upon God's initiative. Humanity cannot save itself, thus the act of election is solely God's doing. This is emphasized in 2 Tim 1:9, where the author reminds us that we have been saved not because of anything we have done, but simply because of God's own purpose and grace.

The writer of Colossians reminds his readers that the *eklektoi*, even though chosen by God's grace, must nonetheless exercise personal responsibility in living a Christian life. As the author puts it, the chosen people must "clothe themselves with compassion, kindness, humility, gentleness and patience" (Col 3:12).

Eleutheros—Freedom

(El-you'-ther-ahs)

Key Passage: Galatians 5:1

Literal Greek: . . .*te eleutheria hemas Christos eleutherosen.* (. . .for *freedom* Christ freed us.)

NAB: It was for liberty that Christ freed us.

JB: When Christ freed us, he meant us to remain free

NEB: Christ set us free, to be free men.

NIV: It is for freedom that Christ has set us free.

Eleutheros is derived from the verb *eleutheroo*, which means "to make free" or "to deliver from bondage." In his Gospel John says that *he aletheia eleutherosei humas*, "the truth will free you" (Jn 8:32). The key passage stresses that freedom is the gift won for humanity by Christ. This is shown in Matthew's story of the Temple tax; its point is that *eleutheroi eisin hoi huioi*, "the sons are free" (Mt 17:26).

Paul refers in his writings to Christian freedom from the Law, as in Rom 7:3, where he uses the analogy of the woman who is *eleuthera* to marry again after the death of her husband. Paul's point is that his readers' marriage to the Law is now ended because Christ has defeated it and given us freedom, our new spouse.

The Christian thus is no longer *doulos*, "slave" (see p. 26), but *eleutheros*, "freeman" (Col 3:11). *Freeman* is a technical term connoting the person who has won his or her freedom after having been the property of another. Paul is saying that Christians are now no longer the property of sin, but freemen; they have been brought out of bondage by Jesus Christ and delivered from their past condition of slavery.

Elpis—Hope

(El-pis′)

Key Passage: Romans 8:24

Literal Greek: *Gar elpidi esothemen elpis de blepomene ouk estin elpis ho gar blepei tis, ti kai elpizei?* (For by *hope* we were saved; but *hope* being seen is not *hope*; for what someone sees why also does he *hope*?)

NAB: In hope we were saved. But hope is not hope if its object is seen; how is it possible for one to hope for what he sees?

JB: For we must be content to hope that we shall be saved—our salvation is not in sight, we should not have to be hoping for it if it were. . . .

NEB: For we have been saved, though only in hope. Now to see is no longer to hope: why should a man endure and wait for what he already sees?

NIV: For in this hope we were saved. But hope that is seen is no hope at all. Who hopes for what he already has?

Elpis means more than simply wishing or desiring. It is the confident anticipation of God's gift of grace and salvation. Hope is essentially *elpidi zoes aionion*, "the hope of eternal life" which is promised by God (Ti 1:2). It is essentially Jesus who is our *elpidos*, as in 1 Tm 1:1. Before the time of Christ, humanity was in a condition of *elpida me echontes* ("not having hope") and thus *atheoi*, "godless" (Eph 2:12).

In Rom 15:4 Paul says that we gain hope through *hupomones* ("patience, endurance") and through the *parakleseos ton graphon* ("comfort of the writings or Scriptures"). Hope has a purifying power rendering the believer more holy and Godlike; see, for example, 1 Jn 3:3, where the author says that everyone having *elpida* . . *hagnizei eauton*, "purifies himself," just as God himself is *hagnos* ("pure").

The related verb is *elpizo*, which sometimes has the connotation of trust. For example, in 2 Cor 1:10 Paul talks about Jesus *eis hon elpikamen*, "in whom we have hope" in the sense of "in whom we have placed our trust." To hope is thus similar to one's having *pepoithesin*, "trust, confidence," as in 2 Cor 3:4.

An interesting related word is *hupostasis* which we will see again in considering faith (see page 114). *Hupostasis* means literally "standing" (*stasis*) "under" (*hupo*), "enduring." In 2 Cor 9:4 Paul is worried that his *hupostasei* ("confidence") in the Corinthians may be misplaced. The author of Heb 3:14 encourages his readers to hold firmly to the *hupostaseos* which they first placed in Christ.

Episkopos—Bishop

(Eh-pis'-kaw-paws)

Key Passage: 1 Timothy 3:2

Literal Greek: ...*dei oun ton episkopon anepilempton einai, mias gunaikos andra, nephalion, sophrona, kosmion, philoxenon*.... (It is necessary therefore that the *bishop* be without reproach, husband of one wife, temperate, sensible, orderly, hospitable....)

NAB: A bishop must be irreproachable, married only once, of even temper, self-controlled, modest and hospitable.

JB: That is why the president must have an impeccable character. He must not have been married more than once....

NEB: Our leader, therefore, or bishop, must be above reproach, faithful to his one wife....

NIV: Now the overseer must be above reproach, the husband of but one wife, temperate....

As the different versions show, the understanding of *episkopos* varies. The word is used in Acts 20:28 where Paul cautions those elders he has appointed in his previous missionary journeys to be prudent "overseers" or "bishops." In Acts 20:17, Luke refers to these same people as *presbuterous tes ekklesias* ("elders" of the Church). Apparently *presbuteros* was the earlier term for the elders and *episkopos* was a later adaptation.

Further, *presbuteros* connotes the gift of maturity and wisdom which a Christian leader possesses, while *episkopos* suggests more his actual function, the duties which the man was to undertake. It was not until the second century that the Church distinguished the two words, applying *episkopos* to what we know today as a "bishop" and

44

presbuteros to the "priests."

The office of bishop is derived from Jesus' own ministry; in 1 Pt 2:25 the author refers to the Lord as *episkopon ton psuchon humon,* "the bishop of your souls." The early Church saw the episcopacy as an important office, as indicated in Acts 1:20, where the apostles discuss replacing Judas's *episkopen* ("office" or "position of leadership").

Epithesis—Laying On

(Eh-pi'-thess-is)

Key Passage: 1 Timothy 4:14

Literal Greek: ...*meta epitheseos ton cheiron tou presbuteriou.* (...with *laying on* of hands of the body of elders.)

NAB: Do not neglect the gift you received when, as a result of prophecy, the presbyters laid their hands on you.

JB: ...the body of elders laid their hands on you...

NEB: ...through the laying on of the hands of the elders as a body.

NIV: ...when the body of elders laid their hands on you.

The early Church (and thus the New Testament) attributed great significance to the act of laying hands on someone. This is seen clearly in Acts 8:18 where Simon the magician, having noticed that the Holy Spirit was given *dia tes epitheseos ton cheiron ton apostolon* ("through the laying on of the hands of the apostles"), tries to no avail to bribe the apostles into giving him the same authority. In Acts 6:6

45

the apostles' new assistants received their commission after the apostles *epethekan autois tas cheiras,* "placed on them their hands."

Epithesis is related to the verb *epitithemi,* "to lay upon." It was the custom of the early Church to lay hands upon the sick in order to heal them. In Mt 9:18 the synagogue ruler begs Jesus to *epithes ten cheira,* "lay hands on" his daughter.

Apparently, the act was seen as identifying the person who performed the action with the person whose body was touched. Therefore laying on of hands transferred authority. Paul reminds Timothy of the day when he imparted his authority to him through *epitheosis ton cheiron mou,* "the laying on of my hands" (2 Tm 1:6).

Euaggelion—Gospel

(You-ahn-jehl'-ion)

Key Passage: Romans 1:16

Literal Greek: ...*ou gar epaischunomia to euaggelion dunamis gar Theou estin eis soterian panti to pisteuonti....* (I am not ashamed of the *gospel;* for it is God's power to salvation to everyone believing....)

NAB: I am not ashamed of the gospel. It is the power of God leading everyone who believes in it to salvation....

JB: For I am not ashamed of the Good News: it is the power of God saving all who have faith....

NEB: For I am not ashamed of the Gospel. It is the saving power of God for everyone who has faith....

NIV: I am not ashamed of the gospel, because it is the power of God for the salvation of everyone who believes....

The origin of *euaggelion* is interesting. In ancient times when a messenger delivered good news to his king, such as word of a victory on some distant battlefield, the king would give the messenger *euaggelion,* a "reward," for his service.

The New Testament evangelists adopted this word for oral and written proclamation of the Good News of Jesus Christ. This usage is reflected in Acts 15:7, where Peter says that God chose him to deliver to the Gentiles *ton logon tou euaggeliou,* "the word of the gospel."

Paul uses the word in both a historical and a doctrinal sense. The first sense is seen in 1 Cor 15:1, where he reminds the Corinthians of *to euaggelion ho euaggelisamen,* "the good news which I preached"—the historical details of the

47

life, teaching and ministry of Jesus Christ. He uses *euaggelion* in a doctrinal sense in Gal 1:9, where he condemns anyone who *euaggelizetai par ho parelabete,* "preaches a gospel besides what you received."

The New Testament writers used several interesting metaphors to refer to the gospel. For example, Paul calls it "the glory of Christ" (2 Cor 4:4) and *charitos tou Theou,* "the grace of God" (Acts 20:24). The writer of Ephesians calls the gospel *ton logon tes aletheias,* "the word of truth" (1:13); in 6:15 he equates the *euaggelion* with *eirenes,* "peace."

Euaggelizo—
To Preach the Gospel

(You-ahn-jehl-eye'-zoe)

Key Passage: Luke 4:18

Literal Greek: "...*ou heineken echrisen me euaggelisasthai ptochois....*" ("Wherefore he anointed me *to preach the good news* to the poor.")

NAB: "The spirit of the Lord is upon me;
    therefore he has anointed me.
  He has sent me to bring glad tidings
    to the poor,
    to proclaim liberty to captives...."

JB: "He has sent me to bring the good news
    to the poor...."

NEB: "...he has sent me to announce good news
    to the poor...."

NIV: "...therefore he has anointed me to preach
    good news to the poor."

48

The verb *euaggelizo* refers to the Good News of the gospel. (The noun *euaggelion*, "gospel," is treated on p. 47.)

A related verb is *kerusso*, "to proclaim"—but not necessarily the Good News. For example, the leper whom Jesus has cured in Mk 1:45 goes out *kerussein*, "to proclaim" what Jesus has just done for him. The related noun is *kerugma*, "proclamation." The early Church adopted this word for the substance of its oral preaching about Jesus. See Rom 16:25, where Paul refers to the *kerugma Iesou Christou*, "the proclamation of Jesus Christ," referring to what he preached *about* Jesus.

Today we use the term *kerygma* to refer to the early Church's *oral* proclamation of Jesus Christ. *Euaggelion*, on the other hand, has come to mean the *written* teaching about Jesus preserved for us in the New Testament. In actuality, however, both words refer to the Church's proclamation of the Good News of Jesus.

In English, a "proclamation" connotes delivering a message orally; we frequently forget that the written word itself is meant to be proclaimed. The Gospels were usually orally proclaimed in the first Christian communities rather than read in private by individuals. It would perhaps help us to return to the original sense and purpose of the Gospels today if they were really proclaimed when they are read in our churches, rather than recited.

Eucharisteo—To Give Thanks

(You-kah-rees-teh'-owe)

Key Passage: Matthew 26:27

Literal Greek: *Kai labon poterion kai eucharistesas edoken autois....* (And taking a cup and *giving thanks* he gave it to them.)

NAB: Then he took a cup, gave thanks, and gave it to them.

JB: Then he took a cup, and when he had returned thanks he gave it to them.

NEB: Then he took a cup, and having offered thanks to God he gave it to them....

NIV: Then he took the cup, gave thanks and offered it to them....

Jesus' act of giving thanks to the Father before he consecrated the cup of the new covenant became such a familiar image to the early Church that it gave a name to the sacrament he instituted. Thus today we have the Eucharist.

The verb *eucharisteo* is common in the New Testament, and does not usually have sacramental significance. Notice, however, that John uses the word in his story of the loaves and fishes. First *eucharistesas* ("having given thanks") Jesus performs the miracle and distributes the loaves (Jn 6:11). By the time Jn was written, the early Church had probably already come to associate *eucharistia* ("thankfulness") with the sacrament.

Aside from this most significant theological usage of *eucharisteo*, the New Testament constantly extols the virtue of thankfulness. At some point in the introduction to each of his letters (except for 2 Cor), Paul gives thanks to God for his readers: e.g., *"eucharisto* (I thank) God for all of you" (Rom 1:8); *"eucharisto* (I thank) God every time I think of you" (Phil 1:3).

One of the New Testament's key verses on thankfulness urges the reader to "sing praise to the Lord with all your hearts, giving thanks always for all things—*eucharistountes pantote huper panton*—in the name of our Lord Jesus Christ" (Eph 5:19-20).

We get some understanding of *eucharisteo* when we compare it to a related verb *exomologeo*, which literally means "to make an acknowledgment," but which is translated in some places as "to give thanks." For example, in Mt 11:25, Jesus says "*exomologoumai*," which is variously translated "I offer praise" (NAB), "I bless you" (JB), "I thank thee" (NEB) and "I praise you" (NIV). Although each of these translations is appropriate, they perhaps do not perfectly express the concept of making an *acknowledgment* of the Father's merciful favor. This latter connotation summarizes the New Testament's understanding of thankfulness: grateful recognition and acknowledgment of the Father's goodness.

Exousia—Authority

(Ex-oo-see'-ah)

Key Passage: Matthew 28:18

Literal Greek: "...*edothe moi pasa exousia en ourano kai epi tes ges.*" ("...was given to me all *authority* in heaven and on the earth.")

NAB: "Full authority has been given to me both in heaven and on earth...."

JB: "All authority in heaven and on earth has been given to me."

NEB: "Full authority in heaven and on earth has been committed to me."

NIV: Identical to JB.

Exousia has two connotations: the concept of lawfulness and the concept of power or ability. In Mt 9:6 these two concepts come together where Jesus says that he has *exousian* to forgive sins: He is lawfully designated by God to forgive sins and has as well the same power in his own person.

Paul's use of the word likewise emphasizes both connotations. He talks about the *exousias,* the "power the Lord has given us for your upbuilding and not for your destruction" (2 Cor 10:8, NAB). The NEB translates *exousias* here as "authority," as do the JB and the NIV. The NAB seems to deemphasize the first connotation of *exousia,* lawful authority. Paul is telling his flock not only that he has the *power* to build up the Church but also that he has been commissioned as an apostle with the *legal right* to do so.

An illustration will perhaps clarify the two connotations. A policeman standing in front of a speeding cement truck has a lawful right to stop the truck from speeding, but not the power. On the other hand, a Latin American dictator who suppresses the legitimate rights of his people has the power but not the legal right.

The New Testament concept of authority combines both power and legal right. For example, through the Holy Spirit Christians not only have the the *legal right* to share in Jesus' sonship and his ministry of reconciliation, they also have the *power* to act as "sons" and to reconcile.

It is important that the Church never lose sight of either connotation, since a Church acting out of power with no lawful authority can be dictatorial, while a Church exercising lawful authority with no power is of no effect in the world. Christians are given true *exousia,* that is, they are endowed with both lawful right and power to continue Jesus' works and his life in the world.

Gennao—Beget, Give Birth To

(Gen [hard G]-ah'-owe)

Key Passage: John 3:3

Literal Greek: "...*ean me tis gennethe anothen, ou dunatai idein ten basileian tou Theou*." ("Except anyone is *begotten* from above, he cannot see the Kingdom of God.")

NAB: "I solemnly assure you, no one can see the reign of God unless he is begotten from above."

JB: "...unless a man is born from above..."

NEB: "...unless a man has been born over again..."

NIV: "...unless a man is born again..."

Gennao suggests "giving birth" or, metaphorically, "making into children." In the key passage the verb is passive and can mean either "to be born" or "to be begotten." The word *anothen*, which literally means "from above," indicates that God's power is necessary to give rebirth to human beings and make them into new, spiritual creatures.

Paul uses the word in 1 Cor 4:15 when he tells the Corinthians that he *egennesa* ("begat") them *dia tou euaggeliou*, "through the gospel." The act of "begetting" thus depended on the preaching of the gospel. This is consistent with Paul's definition of the gospel as "the power of God leading everyone who believes in it to salvation" (Rom 1:16).

Gnosis—Knowledge

(Gun-owé-sis)

Key Passage: Philippians 3:8

Literal Greek: ...*hegoumai panta zemaian einai dia to huperechon tes gnoseos Christou Iesou....* (I deem all things to be loss on account of the excellence of the *knowledge* of Christ Jesus.)

NAB: I have come to rate all as loss in the light of the surpassing knowledge of my Lord Jesus Christ.

JB: ...I believe nothing can happen that will outweigh the supreme advantage of knowing Christ Jesus my Lord.

NEB: ...I count everything sheer loss, because all is far outweighed by the gain of knowing Christ Jesus my Lord....

NIV: ...I consider everything a loss compared to the surpassing greatness of knowing Christ Jesus my Lord....

Gnosis is used frequently in the New Testament to connote awareness of the spiritual reality of Christ in one's life. The highest form of *gnosis*, as well as the highest form of truth, is God himself as revealed in Jesus Christ. Jesus condemns the scribes and Pharisees for taking away from the people the *kleida tes gnoseos*, "key of knowledge" (Lk 11:52), i.e., preventing the people from knowing the true revelation of God in Jesus Christ.

A related word is *epignosis*, which connotes a deeper form of knowledge, something which we could perhaps call intuition—a knowledge that is based not simply on factual data but on one's own experience of the truth of what is perceived.

The writer of Ephesians prays that his readers may come to *epignosei* of God (1:17). The NAB translates this term as "to know him clearly"; it is "full knowledge" in the JB, "knowledge" in the NEB and "so that we may know him better" in the NIV. It is difficult for English to convey fully the sense of *epignosis*.

The related verb—*ginosko*, "to know"—also connotes the deeper sense of knowledge suggested by *epignosis*, i.e., to know deeply through relationship rather than grasping a set of facts. Paul says that if anyone loves God, such a person *egnostai hup autou*, "has been known by him" (1 Cor 8:3) in the sense of intimate relationship.

Another New Testament word for "know" is *oida*. In Jn 6:6 Jesus questions his disciples about bread for the people even though he *edei* ("knew") that he was about to perform a miracle. Paul uses the same verb in 2 Cor 11:31, where he testifies to the truth of his teaching by saying that God *oiden* ("knows") he is not lying.

Hagiasmos—Holiness, Sanctity

(Hah-gee-ahs-maws')

Key Passage: Hebrews 12:14

Literal Greek: ...*kai ton hagiasmon, hou choris oudeis opsetai ton kurion.* (...and for *holiness* without which no one will see the Lord.)

NAB: Strive for peace with all men, and for that holiness without which no one can see the Lord.

JB: ...and the holiness without which no one can ever see the Lord.

NEB: ...and a holy life, for without that no one will see the Lord.

NIV: ...and to be holy; without holiness no one will see the Lord.

Hagiasmos is frequently translated as "sanctification," and thus suggests being *made* holy. Paul makes it clear in 1 Cor 1:30 that Jesus himself *is* our *hagiasmos*, our "holiness" or our "sanctification." Thus it is through Jesus that a person acquires holiness or the ability to draw near to God. In Acts 26:18 Paul recounts that Jesus commissioned him to preach forgiveness of sins to those who are *hegiasmenois pistei*, "having been sanctified by faith." Faith in Jesus makes God's people holy.

In the Church it is the Holy Spirit who brings about this state of sanctification. Even the Gentiles have become acceptable to God, *hegiasmene en pneumati hagio*, "having been sanctified by the Holy Spirit" (Rom 15:16). The author of 1 Pt 1:2 likewise refers to the *hagiasmo pneumatos*, "sanctification of the Spirit." Persons who have thus been sanctified are called the *hagiois*, "saints," as in 2 Thes 1:10.

The corresponding adjective *hagios* ("holy") refers principally to God. In Jewish thinking God himself was the only Holy One. Luke reminds us of this in the Magnificat, where Mary says *hagion to onoma autou*, "holy is the name of him [God]" (1:49).

Although the act of sanctification is principally the work of God through his Spirit, human beings themselves must participate in the act of being made holy. The writer of 1 Pt admonishes his readers to become *hagioi en pase anastrophe*, "holy in all conduct" (1:15). By cooperating with God's gift of sanctification Christians become *heirateuma hagion*, "a holy priesthood" (1 Pt 2:50), and *ethnos hagion*, "a holy nation" (1 Pt 2:9).

Hagios should be distinguished from *hieros* or "sacred" as in 2 Tm 3:15, where the writer refers to the Old Testament as *hiera grammata*, "sacred letters." *Hagios* is also distinct from *hagnos* ("pure"), as in Phil 4:8, where the author admonishes his readers to keep their thoughts on *hosa hagna*, "whatever are pure things." *Hagios* suggests a higher good than either *hieros* or *hagnos*. Its principal connotation is being made like to God. It thus encompasses both *hieros* and *hagnos*, while suggesting a more Godlike state than the other two words.

Hamartia—Sin

(Hahm-are-tee'-ah)

Key Passage: Romans 5:12

Literal Greek: *Dia touto hosper di enos anthropou he hamartia eis ton kosmon eiselthen, kai dia tes hamartias ho thanatos....* (Therefore, as through one man *sin* entered into the world and through *sin* death....)

NAB: Therefore, just as through one man sin entered the world and with sin death....

JB: Well then, sin entered the world through one man, and through sin death....

NEB: It was through one man that sin entered the world, and through sin death....

NIV: Therefore, just as sin entered the world through one man, and death through sin....

As the key passage suggests, *hamartia* should not be thought of as an action, but as a *force* producing evil actions. The actions we call sins are the *symptoms* of sin. Paul makes this clear elsewhere, where he says everyone is *huph hamartian*, "under sin" (Rom 3:9), i.e., under the power of a principle or law which governs humanity's behavior. *Hamartia* holds sway unless and until a countervailing power intervenes to eradicate it.

Hamartia was overcome on the cross when God *epoiesen* ("made," in the sense of "allowed him to become") Christ *hamartian* (2 Cor 5:21). The power of *hamartia* could only be defeated by being put to death in the person of Jesus Christ, who became sin on our behalf, destroying it in his own body as he died on the cross.

For Christians who incorporate themselves into Christ through faith, sin is thus an ever-dying force which inevitably must succumb to the life-giving power of Jesus' Resurrection.

58

As Paul puts it, "If we have died with Christ, we believe that we are also to live with him. We know that Christ, once raised from the dead, will never die again; death has no more power over him. His death was death to sin, once for all; his life is life for God. In the same way, you must consider yourselves dead to sin but alive for God in Christ Jesus" (Rom 6:8-11, NAB).

Although the New Testament does use *hamartia* to refer to bad conduct (in Acts 7:60, Stephen refers to the Jews' stoning him as *hamartian*), a more precise word for sinful behavior is *hamartema*. We see this usage in Mk 3:28, where Jesus says that all *ta hamartemata*, "the sins," will be forgiven people, except blasphemy against the Holy Spirit.

Perhaps a more accurate understanding of sin as bad conduct is suggested by the Greek word for "trespass" or "transgression" as in Eph 1:7, where Paul says through the blood of Jesus we have forgiveness *ton paraptomaton*, "of trespasses." *Paraptoma* literally means a "false step" or a "fall beside." It is the result or symptom of *hamartia*. Humanity, not yet fully freed from the power of *hamartia*, continually takes *paraptomaton*, "false steps."

Interestingly, Matthew uses the word *opheilemata* ("debts") as a synonym for sins. His version of the Lord's Prayer asks God to "forgive us our debts" ("forgive us the wrong we have done" in the NAB), while Luke's version says "forgive us our *hamartias* (sins)" (Lk 11:4).

Matthew's version focuses more on day-to-day transgressions. Luke, on the other hand, focuses more on the forgiveness for a life not yet surrendered completely to the liberating power of Jesus' Resurrection, that is, a life which still clings to the power and allurement of *hamartia*.

Notice that Luke's version does not include "but deliver us from the evil one" (Mt 6:13b). Rather, Luke closes with "and lead us not into temptation" (or "subject us not to the [Endtime] trial" in the NAB; Lk 11:14). Luke's focus on *hamartia* extends to the Christian's Endtime deliverance from its destructive power.

Hiereus—Priest

(He-err-yous')

Key Passage: Hebrews 4:15

Literal Greek: *...ou gar echomen archierea me dunamenon sumpathesai tais astheneiais hemon....* (For we do not have a high *priest* not being able to suffer with our weakness....)

NAB: For we do not have a high priest who is unable to sympathize with our weakness, but one who was tempted in every way that we are, yet never sinned.

JB: For it is not as if we had a high priest who was incapable of feeling our weaknesses with us....

NEB: For ours is not a high priest unable to sympathize with our weaknesses....

NIV: For we do not have a high priest who is unable to sympathize with our weaknesses....

Hiereus (the key passage has the variation *archiereaus*) literally means "one who offers sacrifice." The priests of the old covenant offered sacrifices to God year after year in hopes of satisfying their debt to God for sin. By his death Jesus performed the perfect act of sacrifice, and it is in this sense that the New Testament refers to him as *hiereus*.

The Christian priesthood is a continuation of the priesthood of Jesus Christ—not in the sense that Christian priests *add* anything to Jesus' sacrifice, but in that they are ministers who *continue* the ongoing effects of that sacrifice into the present moment. The Christian priest does this by celebrating the sacrifice of the Mass, the reintegration into time of Calvary.

Besides the specifically ministerial priesthood, the New

Testament designates *all* Christians, laity included, as priests. The author of 1 Pt refers to the body of believers as *hierateuma hagion* or "a holy priesthood" (2:5). The meaning of this priesthood is seen in Rom 12:1, where Paul asks his readers to present their bodies as *thusian zosan,* "a living sacrifice." All Christians, to the extent to which they offer themselves to God sacrificially, dying on their personal crosses for the continuing salvation of humanity, are priests.

Christians continue the most fundamental calling which God gave to his people in earliest times when he made them "a kingdom of priests, a holy nation" (Ex 19:6). The special vocation of the ancient Israelites was to serve as priests to the nations, to offer sacrifices to God for humanity by keeping themselves holy for the good of all creation. Christians continue this ministry insofar as they sacrifice themselves for the good of humanity.

Huios—Son

(Hwee-aws')

Key Passage:	John 8:36
Literal Greek:	*"Ean oun ho huios humas eleutherose, ontos eleutheroi osotha."* ("If therefore the Son frees you, really free you will be.")
NAB:	"That is why, if the son frees you, you will really be free."
JB:	"So if the Son makes you free, you will be free indeed."
NEB:	"If then the Son sets you free, you will indeed be free."
NIV:	"So if the Son sets you free, you will be free indeed."

Although the New Testament uses *huios* in its ordinary sense of male offspring, as where Paul writes that Abraham had *duo huious*, "two sons" (Gal 4:22), the principal theological significance of *huios* is much more profound. We get a hint of this in Matthew's version of the Beatitudes, where Jesus says that the peacemakers will be called *huioi Theou*, "sons of God" (Mt 5:9).

Huios in its principal theological significance does not mean a male child of God as opposed to God's female child. The Greek word for "child" is *teknon;* see Jn 1:12, where the author refers to those who have received Jesus as *tekna Theou*, "children of God." There is a difference between the New Testament understanding of "children of God" and "sons of God." Paul writes that "all who are led by the Spirit of God *huioi eisin Theou*, are sons of God" (Rom 8:14). The indwelling Spirit transforms men and women into the very likeness of God's own incarnate Word, the preexistent Son, the same Son of glory who reigns forever at the right hand of the Father. To be called a "son" of God in this sense connotes something much fuller than being called a "child" of God.

To say that we are *huioi Theou*, "sons of God," in this higher sense means that both men *and* women are "sons." This is one place in the New Testament where neuterizing the Greek word, substituting "children" or "offspring" for "sons," destroys the underlying theological significance.

This higher theological significance of *huios* in no way slights women by calling them "sons" rather than "daughters." In Christ *ouk eni arsen kai thelu*, "there cannot be male and female" (Gal 3:28). Paul's point is that in Christ all people, men and women alike, have been raised to the status of the Son; they share in the most intimate way possible the divine interrelationship between God the Father and the divine Son.

Women are daughters of God in the sense that they are of equal status with men in the order of human creation, but they are not daughters in the ultimate fulfillment of God's eternal plan. Rather, they too are *huios*, an entirely new genderless creation sharing the divinity of Father and

Son. To use the word *huios* for this new status is perhaps inadequate, but the New Testament gives us no other alternative. To substitute "child" or "daughter" would be to underestimate the exalted status we all have in Christ.

Huiothesia—Adoption

(Hwee-ah-thess-ee'-ah)

Key Passage: Romans 8:15

Literal Greek: ...*alla elabete pneuma huiothesias*....
(...but you received a spirit of *adoption*....)

NAB: You did not receive a spirit of slavery leading you back into fear, but a spirit of adoption through which we cry out, "Abba" (that is, "Father!").

JB: ...it is the spirit of sons....

NEB: ...a Spirit that makes us sons....

NIV: ...the Spirit who makes you sons....

Huiothesia is a combination of two words: *huios*, "son," and *thesis*, "placing." Thus the word literally means "giving to someone the place of a son." Notice that Paul in Romans says that we have received a *pneuma* ("spirit") of adoption. This is the work of the Holy Spirit, who enables Christians to realize and proclaim their new status as "sons."

The writer of Ephesians continues this thought when he says that God "predestined us through Jesus Christ to be his adopted sons"; literally, "predestinating us *eis huiothesian* (to adoption of sons) through Jesus Christ" (1:5). Notice that the Greek suggests the concept of sonship, not childhood.

63

Huiothesia does not connote the same thing as becoming "children" of God, but rather being placed into a position of sonship, which is a higher gift in the sense that it transforms human nature into the very nature of the Son (see *Huios,* p. 61). Thus, *huiothesia* is seen by Paul (the only New Testament writer to use this word) as the pinnacle of the Christian's calling.

Paul emphasizes this when he says that we are still "eagerly expecting our *huiothesian,*" which he equates with "the redemption of our bodies" (Rom 8:23). Although our *huiothesia* has been effected by the Holy Spirit, it has not yet come to fruition.

Hupakoe—Obedience

(Hew-pah-kaw-ay')

Key Passage: Hebrews 5:8

Literal Greek: *Kaiper on huios, emathen aph on epathen ten hupakone....* (Though being a son, he learned from things which he suffered *obedience....*)

NAB: Son though he was, he learned obedience from what he suffered....

JB: Although he was Son, he learned to obey through suffering....

NEB: ...son though he was, he learned obedience in the school of suffering....

NIV: Although he was a son, he learned obedience from what he suffered....

Hupakoe comes from *akouo* ("to hear") and *hupo* ("under"); literally, "to hear under." The point of the key passage is that

Jesus "heard under" the Father's word, or obeyed it, through suffering. In the same way, Christians are called to "hear under" God's will even through suffering.

A related word which conveys the same meaning is *hupotage*, which comes from *tasso* ("to order") and *hupo* ("under")—"to order under." In 2 Cor 9:13 Paul writes of the *hupotage* ("submission" or "subjection") of his readers to the gospel. (The word is translated as "obedient faith" in the NAB.)

The related verb *hupakouo*, which means "to listen," has the connotation of listening *and* submitting. For example, when Jesus calmed the winds and the waves, these elements of nature were said by the apostles to *hupakouousin*, "hear" or "obey" Jesus. Perhaps we could say that *hupakouo* means "heed" as well as "hear." For example, in Acts 6:7 we read that many priests *hupekouon te pistei*, "heard the faith"—or, as the NAB has it, "embraced the faith."

Iesous—Jesus

(Ee-yay'-soos)

Key Passage: Luke 1:31

Literal Greek: "...*kai kaleseis to onoma autou Iesoun*." ("...and you shall call the name of him Jesus.")

NAB: "You shall conceive and bear a son and give him the name Jesus."

JB: "...and you must name him Jesus."

NEB: "...and you shall give him the name Jesus."

NIV: "...and you are to give him the name Jesus."

Iesous comes from the Hebrew *Joshua*, which means "Yahweh is salvation," a common name among the Jews of Jesus' time. In Luke's genealogy, one of Jesus' ancestors is referred to as "Joshua, son of Eliezer" (3:29); in Greek the spelling is *Iesou*.

In the Epistles the name *Iesous* is rarely used by itself, but in conjunction with another title such as *Lord* or *Christ*.

The title *Jesus Christ* occurs in Mt 1:1; 1:18 and 16:21; in Jn 1:17 and 17:3. In Mark's Gospel it appears only in the opening verse. In Acts the most frequent usage is *tou kuriou Iesou*, "the Lord Jesus" (see Acts 8:16).

Interestingly, Paul reverses the order of the title, preferring "Christ Jesus." Perhaps this is because Paul never knew Jesus of Nazareth, the man, but experienced Jesus only in his risen power as the Christ of salvation. Paul exhorts the Philippians to have the same attitude as that of *Christo Iesou* (Phil 2:5); yet in 2:11 says that every tongue shall proclaim *kurios Iesous Christos* ("Jesus Christ is Lord"). Scholars think that Paul makes use of a very early Christian hymn in Phil 2:6-11. This could explain why in this passage he uses the earlier "Jesus Christ" instead of his own preference, "Christ Jesus."

Kainos—New

(Kie [rhymes with pie]-naws')

Key Passage:	Revelation 21:5
Literal Greek:	*"Idou kaina poio panta."* ("Behold, *new* I make all things.")
NAB:	"...See, I make all things new!"
JB:	"...Now I am making the whole of creation new...."
NEB:	"...Behold! I am making all things new!"
NIV:	"...I am making everything new!"

Kainos connotes "new" in the sense of a transformation of something that has already existed. It does not connote the creation or sudden appearance of something that has never existed before. In one sense, the entire New Testament is a study in the theology of "newness."

In John's Gospel Jesus says that he has given an *entolen kainen*, "new commandment" (Jn 13:34). For Paul, the very essence of Christianity is that one becomes *kaine ktisis*, "a new creation" (Gal 6:15); it was to describe the process by which one is born anew that Paul wrote much of his theology.

Another New Testament word for "new," *neos*, is perhaps synonymous with "recent." Whereas *kainos* connotes a transformation so radical that what is remade no longer has its previous characteristics, *neos* suggests that this remaking or transformation has just begun.

For example, the *kainon anthropon* ("new man") of Eph 2:15 is a person who has been radically transformed into a new spiritual creature, existing in a radically new state of consciousness. In contrast, Col 3:10 refers to putting on *ton neon* ("the new person"). In the same passage the writer says that this new person is *anakainoumenon*, "being renewed." In other words, the renewal has just begun.

67

Another example of the two different conceptions of newness is found in the comparison of the *oinon neon* ("new wine") of Mt 9:17, and the wine which Jesus will drink *kainon* ("new") in the Kingdom of God (Mk 14:25). The first new wine is recently fermented, whereas the new wine of the Kingdom is a radically transformed, entirely different type of wine.

Kairos—Time

(Kie-raws')

Key Passage: Romans 5:6

Literal Greek: *Ei ge Christos onton hemon asthenon eti kata kairon huper asebon apethanen.*
(Indeed, Christ, our being weak, yet according to *time* on behalf of godless ones died.)

NAB: At the appointed time, when we were still powerless, Christ died for us godless men.

JB: We were still helpless when at his appointed moment Christ died for sinful men.

NEB: For at the very time when we were still powerless, then Christ died for the wicked.

NIV: You see, at just the right time, when we were still powerless, Christ died for the ungodly.

Although it departs substantially from the literal Greek, the JB translation best preserves the sense of *kairos* in this verse. As we shall see, the New Testament used several words for "time." The best way to understand *kairos* is perhaps by thinking of it as "vertical time" or perhaps "universal time." *Kairos* refers not to a particular hour or minute, day, week or month, but to God's full presence in the material dimension of reality.

Kairos is best understood in contrast to another common New Testament word for "time": *chronos*. *Chronos* connotes time in its more ordinary sense: a duration or period definitely marked by certain limits. For example, in Mt 2:7 Herod inquires of the Magi the *chronon* that the star had appeared in the sky. Herod wishes to know the precise hour so that he can make astrological calculations to determine the meaning of the mysterious star. Another example of *chronos* occurs in Acts 20:18, where Paul reminds the elders of the Church of Ephesus how he was with them *ton panta chronon*, "the whole time." These two examples illustrate that *chronos* is time as we ordinarily think of it today.

Kairos, on the other hand, is a time which is more expressive of God's plan and purpose. We see *chronos* and *kairos* used together in Acts 1:7, where Jesus tells his disciples that it is not for them to know the *chronous e kairous* ("times or moments") when the Father is going to restore his rule in Israel. By using both *chronos* and *kairos* here, Jesus is saying, in effect, "It is not for you to know the day, month, and year when I will return in glory, nor is it for you to perceive the full scope of my Father's plan."

Paul expressed the same idea in 1 Thes 5:1. He told the Thessalonians he did not need to write to them "as regards *ton chronon kai ton kairon* ("specific times and moments," NAB). The NAB translation here is a good one since it translates *chronon* as "specific time" in the sense of a particular moment on the clock, as it were, and *kairon* as "moment" in the sense of a certain era or epoch in the history of humanity.

Paul is telling his readers, in effect, "you will be able to determine the time when Jesus will come again neither in the sense of the day, month and year nor by trying to guess from the 'signs of the times.'" As the verses following show, neither "peace and security" nor any other outward sign will be an infallible criterion by which to judge the fulfillment of God's plan for humanity.

Another word for time is *hora*, sometimes translated as

"hour." We see an example of this in Mt 14:15, where the disciples, upon seeing the large crowd without food, tell Jesus that *he hora ede parelthen*, "the hour already passed" or, as the NAB has it, "it is already late."

Kaleo—Call

(Kahl-eh'-owe)

Key Passage: Romans 8:30

Literal Greek: ...*hous de proorisen toutous kai ekalesen, kai hous ekalesen, toutous kai edikaiosen....* (But those whom he fore-ordained, these also he *called*; and those whom he *called*, these also he justified.)

NAB: Those he predestined he likewise called; those he called he also justified....

JB: He called those he intended for this; those he called he justified....

NEB: ...and it is these, so foreordained, whom he has also called. And those whom he called he has justified....

NIV: And those he predestined, he also called; those he called, he also justified....

The most rudimentary sense of *kaleo* in the New Testament is God's call to share in the divine life given humanity by Jesus Christ. Paul emphasizes this in 1 Cor 1:9, where he says that we are *eklethete eis koinonian*, "called into fellowship" with Jesus Christ. Hebrews 9:15 refers to Christians as *keklemenoi*, "having been called" to a divine inheritance.

There are interesting variations of *kaleo* which play on

the theme of this fundamental call to a divine inheritance. For example, there is *epikaleo*, which means to be called by a person's name. Jas 2:7 criticizes the rich for blaspheming the name by which Christians are *epiklethen eph humas*, literally, "called on you," or as the NAB paraphrases, "that noble name which has made you God's own."

There is also *metakaleo*, "call for" or "send for." In Acts 7:14 Stephen refers to Joseph's *metekalesato*, act of calling Jacob and his kindred to come into Egypt.

Also related to *kaleo* is *eklego*, to "pick out" or "select." Mk 13:20 refers to those who will be saved as *tous eklektous*, "the chosen" (see p. 40), and in Lk 6:13 Jesus' call to the Twelve is phrased as *eklexamenos*, "choosing."

Another interesting use of *kaleo* is found in the word *paraklesis*, which literally means "to call beside," to call a person to one's side. The word has come to mean "comfort" or "consolation." In Lk 2:25 Simeon is said to be awaiting the *paraklesin*, literally, the "calling of Israel to the side of God" or, more simply, the "consolation" of Israel. In the Beatitudes Jesus warns the rich because they have already received their *paraklesin* (Lk 6:24).

The early Church assigned to the Holy Spirit the role of giving Christians this *paraklesei*, "comfort" (see Acts 9:31). The Spirit became known as the *parakletos*, a word which suggests the power to console or give aid. At the time of Jesus *parakletos* was applied to legal counsel or advocates who were able to give assistance and comfort to people brought before a court of law. In 1 Jn 2:1 the author refers to the *parakleton*, "advocate," who in a sense argues our case before the Father.

The disciples looked upon Jesus himself as a comforter. In Jn 14:16 Jesus refers to *allon parakleton*, "*another* comforter" he would send to his disciples after he had left this world.

Kardia—Heart

(Kar-dee'-ah)

Key Passage: Luke 12:34

Literal Greek: *". . . hopou gar estin ho thesauros humon, ekei kai he kardia humon estai."* ("For where is your treasure, there also your *heart* will be.")

NAB: "Wherever your treasure lies, there your heart will be."

JB,NEB,NIV: Virtually identical to NAB.

As the key passage shows, *kardia* symbolizes a person's innermost feelings, emotions and judgments. It is the human *kardia* which must be reformed so that God's Spirit can make humanity into a new creation.

Jesus constantly had to contend with the Jews' reliance on externals and their superficial observance of the Law. He tried to get the Jews to see that it was not externals, but the interior disposition of one's *kardia* which was important to God. For example, in Mt 15:19 Jesus says *ek gar tes kardias*, "for out of the heart" (translated "mind" in the NAB) come all sorts of evil conduct.

The early Church itself grappled with this distinction between externals and the interior element of life when it debated the question of admitting Gentiles into its ranks— those who were, by Law, impure. At the Council of Jerusalem Peter convinced his fellow Jewish Christians to accept Gentiles into the fold because, as Peter put it, *te pistei katharisas tas kardias auton,* "by faith cleansing their hearts" (Acts 15:9) God had rendered Jew and Gentile alike pure in his sight.

Two related concepts, sometimes difficult to distinguish from *kardia*, are *psuche* ("soul" or "life") and *nous* ("mind").

The ordinary sense of *psuche* is "life," as in Mt 2:20 where the angel tells Joseph in a dream to return to Israel with the Christ Child because those who were *zetountes ten psuchen tou paidiou* ("seeking the *life* of the child") are dead.

Yet in Mt 11:29 Jesus tells his listeners to take his yoke upon them in order to find *anapausin tas psuchais humon,* "rest to your souls." The meaning of *psuchais* here is very close to *kardia;* Matthew seems to be referring to the inner life of emotions and feelings.

The almost synonymous meaning of *kardia* and *psuche* is also seen in Eph 6:6, where the writer urges his readers to do the will of God *ek psuches,* "from the soul," which actually seems to mean "with all your heart," the translation given in the NAB.

Nous can likewise connote feeling and emotions, but usually refers to perceiving, understanding and decision-making. For example, on the road to Emmaus Jesus *dienoixen auton ton noun,* "opened up the mind of them" (Lk 24:45). Notice how Luke reserves *nous* for "understanding" and *kardia* for "believing." In Lk 24:25 Jesus chides the disciples for being *bradeis te kardia tou pisteuein,* "slow in heart to believe."

Paul saw *nous* as the battleground for one's conversion. In Rom 7:23 he says that the law of the flesh wars against *to nomo tou noos,* "the law of the mind"; in 7:25 he thanks God that he *to men noi,* "with one mind" serves the law of God. Elsewhere Paul urges the Romans to be transformed *te anakainosei tou noos,* "by the renewing of the mind" (Rom 12:2).

Finally, *pneuma* or "spirit" can also be used to refer to the interior, immaterial dimension of a person. See, for example, Lk 8:55 where Jesus raises Jairus's daughter and *epestrepsen to pneuma autes,* "returned the spirit of her."

There is a certain amount of ambiguity in New Testament use of this term, as we see in Mt 5:3 where the evangelist refers to *hoi ptochoi to pneumati,* "the poor in spirit," by which he means of course those whose *hearts* are disposed toward poverty.

Paul uses *pneuma* frequently. As we have seen, he encourages people to be transformed by renewing their *nous,* "mind." This new state of living in a renewed mind (or in a higher state of consciousness, as we might say) is known as living *kata pneuma*, "according to the Spirit" (Rom 8:5). Paul shows the interplay between *nous* and *pneuma* in Rom 8:6 where he refers to the *phronema tes sarkos* as death. *Phronema* literally means "striving," but the usage here is the same as "mind." Paul is saying that the mind of the flesh brings death, but the *phronema tou pneumatos*, "mind (striving) of the Spirit" brings life and peace. (This verse is so difficult to translate that the NAB, for example, gives a very free interpretation to what Paul actually says.)

The difference in Rom 8:5 between *pneuma* (our human spirit) and *pneumatos* (the Holy Spirit) leads into a discussion of the Third Person of the Trinity, an entirely different subject (see page 117).

Katallage—Reconciliation

(Kah-tah-lah-gay')

Key Passage: Romans 5:11

Literal Greek: *. . . di ou nun ten katallagen elabomen.*
(. . . through whom now the *reconciliation* we received.)

NAB: . . . We go so far as to make God our boast through our Lord Jesus Christ, through whom we have now received reconciliation.

JB: . . . through whom we have already gained our reconciliation.

NEB: . . . through whom we have now been granted reconciliation.

NIV: . . . through whom we have now received reconciliation.

84

The KJV has "atonement" in place of "reconciliation." The basic idea behind *katallage* is that of exchanging a state of enmity for a state of friendship. Perhaps atonement, literally "at-one-ment," expresses this as well as if not better than "reconciliation."

In 2 Cor 5:18-19 Paul defines the concept of *katallage* more clearly. He refers to God as "*katallaxantos* (having reconciled) us to himself through Christ and having given to us the ministry of *katallages*." He goes on to explain that in Christ God was *katallasson eauto* ("reconciling believers to himself"), "not *reckoning* to them their trespasses, and placing in us the word of reconciliation." The word for "reckoning" here is *logizomenos*, translated in the NAB as "not counting against them"; in the JB, "not holding men's faults against them"; and in the NEB, "no longer holding men's misdeeds against them."

The translations accurately convey the idea that God did not treat humanity as its sins deserved but, rather, mercifully placed humanity in a state of *katallage* with God. The passage from 2 Cor 5 also emphasizes that Christians are expected to continue God's work of reconciliation among others. That is, Christians are expected not to hold others' faults against them, but to reconcile with them mercifully and compassionately even when strict justice might dictate otherwise.

Koinonia—
Communion, Fellowship

(Coin-oh-nee'-ah)

Key Passage: Acts 2:42

Literal Greek: ...*esan de proskarterountes te didache ton apostolon kai te koinonia, te klasei tou artou kai tais proseuchais.* (And they were continuing steadfastly in the teaching of the apostles and in the *fellowship*, in the breaking of the loaf, and of the prayers.)

NAB: They devoted themselves to the apostles' instruction and the communal life, to the breaking of bread and the prayers.

JB: These remained faithful to the teaching of the apostles, to the brotherhood, to the breaking of bread and to the prayers.

NEB: They met constantly to hear the apostles' teach, and to share the common life, to break bread, and to pray.

NIV: They devoted themselves to the apostles' teaching and to the fellowship, and to the breaking of bread and to prayer.

Koinonia was one of the most noticeable features of the early Christian body. In the early days of persecution it was said of them, "See how these Christians love one another." The word *koinonia* comes from *koinos* ("common") and *koinoneo*, a verb meaning "to share in" or "to communicate." Thus *koinonia* connotes a common sharing or a common communication.

In Gal 2:9, Paul writes of the hand of *koinonias* ("fellowship") offered to him by Peter, James and John. This understanding of fellowship or communion among Christians reflects fellowship with Jesus himself, as in 1 Cor 1:9 where

86

Paul reminds his readers that they were called to *koinonian* with God through Jesus Christ.

Christians' continuing fellowship with Jesus is expressed sacramentally in the Eucharist, as Paul emphasizes in 1 Cor 10:16, where he reminds the Corinthians that the Eucharistic cup is *koinonia tou haimatos tou Christou*, "a communion of the blood of Christ."

The evangelists stated that one of their purposes for writing was to assist the reader to have *koinonian* with the body of believers. This fellowship is identical to the *koinonia* shared by the Father and the Son (1 Jn 1:3).

It is interesting to note that the concept of fellowship or communion was so important to the early Church that Paul in Rom 15:26 uses *koinonian* to refer to the "contribution" (NAB) which the Churches made to the needy of their day. Thus the early Church saw *koinonia* not simply as a spiritual fellowship of Christians with God or with each other, but a very practical and helpful "communion." See, for example, Heb 13:16, *tes de eupoiias kai koinonias me epilanthanesthe*, "Be not forgetful of doing good and *sharing*" (translated "generosity" in the NAB).

Kosmos—World

(Kawś-maws)

Key Passage: John 3:16

Literal Greek: *...houtos gar egapesen ho Theos ton kosmon...* (*...for thus loved God the world...*)

NAB: Yes, God so loved the world that he gave his only Son, that whoever believes in him may not die but may have eternal life.

JB,NEB,NIV: Virtually identical to NAB.

The key passage abundantly illustrates that "the world" is not something despicable in God's eyes, but rather something that he loves and wishes to bring to a state of happiness.

Yet, left to its own devices, the world will exist in a constant state of opposition to God and to all that is good. Thus, while John wrote that God loved the world, he at the same time understood that the world unsubmitted to God is in grave peril. It is precisely because Jesus reveals to the world its state of separation and alienation from God that the world's values are irrevocably opposed to the values of Jesus' Kingdom.

This is clearly seen in Jn 7:7, where Jesus says that the *kosmos* will hate his disciples just as it hated him, because *ego marturo peri autou hoti ta erga autou ponera estin*, "because I witness about it that its works are evil," or, according to the NAB, "because of the evidence I bring against it/that what it does is evil."

Thus we see that although the world in itself is good and beloved of God, nonetheless it cannot achieve happiness unless it submits to the Lordship of Jesus Christ. Such an act of submission will bring great turmoil to the world as it dies to its own values. In the process, Jesus' disciples will endure great sufferings as the world struggles to maintain its values in the face of the gospel message.

Thus it should come as no surprise to Christians who work to eliminate social injustice, legalized abortion, the suicidal nuclear arms race and other worldly evils that they will be severely rebuked and persecuted. *"Ei ho kosmos humas misei*, if the world hates you," Jesus reminds us, "know it has hated me before you" (Jn 15:18).

It is with this understanding of *kosmos* as the antithesis of God's values that we should consider that statement which is so pertinent to "upwardly mobile," affluent Americans: "What profit would a man show *ean ton kosmon holon kerdese*, if the whole world he should gain and destroy himself in the process?" (Mt 16:26).

Kurios—Lord

(Koor'-yaws)

Key Passage:	Acts 2:36
Literal Greek:	"...*kai kurion auton kai Christon epoiesen ho Theos, touton ton Iesoun hon humeis estaurosate.*" (..."God made both *Lord* and Christ this Jesus whom you crucified.")
NAB:	"Therefore let the whole house of Israel know beyond any doubt that God has made both Lord and Messiah this Jesus whom you crucified."
JB:	"For this reason the whole House of Israel can be certain that God has made this Jesus whom you crucified both Lord and Christ."
NEB:	"Let all Israel then accept as certain that God has made this Jesus, whom you crucified, both Lord and Messiah."
NIV:	"Therefore, let all Israel be assured of this: God has made this Jesus whom you crucified both Lord and Christ."

Perhaps the most astonishing and scandalizing element of the early Christians' proclamation concerning Jesus was their statement that he was *kurios*. To the Jews who did not accept Jesus this was blasphemy, since the title was reserved only for Yahweh, the transcendent God of the entire universe. Jesus himself used this title for God the Father (see Mt 4:7, where Jesus rebukes the devil by telling him not to tempt *kurion ton Theon sou*, "the Lord your God").

The word *kurios* does not necessarily have religious significance; it can mean "sir," "master" or "owner." In Lk 19:33 the owners of the colt which Jesus sends his disciples to fetch are called *hoi kurioi*, "owners," of the colt. One of the more common connotations of *kurios* is seen in Acts

89

25:26, where the Roman official Festus refers to the emperor as *to kurio*, "the Lord."

The word was also used as a polite form of address to a stranger, as in Jn 12:21 where the Greeks address Philip as *kurie*, "Lord" or "sir." Thus, not everywhere in the New Testament where Jesus is referred to as *kurios* does the title imply divinity. For example, in Mt 8:2, where the leper addresses Jesus as *kurie*, it is simply a polite form of address.

Nevertheless, when the early Church said that God had made Jesus "Lord," it was clear that they meant Jesus' divinity by the term. It was this which so angered the Jewish religious establishment and continually got the early evangelists into trouble with them. Matthew portrays Jesus himself as appropriating the title in 7:21, where Jesus rebukes those who call him *kurie, kurie*—"Lord, Lord"—without doing the work of his heavenly Father. Perhaps the theological significance of *kurios* is clearest in Jn 20:28, where Thomas addresses Jesus as *ho kurios mou kai ho Theos mou*, "my Lord and my God."

The early Church thus adapted and completely transformed the ordinary connotation of *kurios* so that it became the principal title by which the Church referred to Jesus' divinity. As the early Church itself discovered, however, no one can say *Kurios Iesous, ei me en pneumati hagio*, that is, no one can know or say that Jesus is Lord "except by the Holy Spirit" (1 Cor 12:3). Only by God's divine insight can one realize that Jesus himself fully partakes of the Father's divinity.

Logos—Word

(Law'-gaws)

Key Passage: John 1:1

Literal Greek: *Theos en ho logos....* (God was the
Word ...)

NAB: ...the Word was God.

JB, NIV: Virtually identical to NAB.

NEB: ...what God was, the Word was.

One could write an entire book simply on the meaning and
significance of the word *word* in the New Testament. The
more familiar and more common term is *logos*; we will
consider *rhema* on p. 120.

Logos is used in many ways in the New Testament.
When the centurion tells Jesus not to bother coming to his
home, but to say only the *logo* so as to cure his servant (Lk
7:7), he is asking not for a spoken word but a mental
command.

Logos can stand for a maxim or ideal. In Gal 5:14 Paul
writes that the entire law can be summarized in one *logo*,
"You shall love your neighbor as yourself." Paul also used
logos to refer to any revelation which he wanted to pass
along to his flock, as in 1 Thes 4:15 where he says that he
instructs his readers *en logo kuriou*, "by a word of the
Lord." Several times when Paul wants to emphasize the
trustworthiness of a particular bit of advice he gives, he
refers to *ho logos* ("the word"). For example, in 1 Tm 3:1 he
says *pistos ho logos* ("faithful is the word"), translated "you
can depend on this" in the NAB.

By far the most theologically significant use of *logos* in
the New Testament occurs in John's Gospel. He equates *logos*
with the Son of God. In the Prologue to his Gospel John
says *en arche en ho logos*, "in the beginning was the Word"
(Jn 1:1), referring of course to the preexistent Word of
God, the Second Person of the Trinity who became flesh in

91

Jesus Christ. In Jn 1:1 the author uses *logos* in this same context, referring to *logou tes zoes*, "the word of life."

John and his school of disciples did not invent *logos* as a synonym for the divine Word; it was a common term in Greek and Roman philosophy. The Stoics in particular had long used the concept of *logos* to refer to the creative principle within the universe. Students of Platonism (the philosophy of Plato) had used a similar concept, the *demiurge*, to express their understanding of how God related to the world and how he created the world's various elements.

The essential difference between these philosophical understandings of *logos* and John's use of the term is that the ancient philosophers conceived of the *logos* as a "lesser God," an intermediate being between God and creation. During the time in which John wrote several schools of thought saw the *logos* as evil. It was thought that the *logos* as creator had brought into existence something which the supreme God would not have chosen had he not been tricked or mistakenly allowed creation to take place.

John, on the other hand, makes it clear that the *logos* is in no way of a lesser order of being than the Father himself: *Theos en ho logos*, "God was the Word" (Jn 1:1). Notice that the English translations reverse the order of the Greek. That is because the English verb *to be* does not adequately convey the dynamic quality of the Greek *einai* ("to be"), which connotes "*making* be." Thus the Greek in the key passage really means "God '*be's*' the Word," i.e., the Word eternally *is* from the Father. This is what the NEB is struggling to convey with its unique translation of the key passage.

Whereas some of the pagan philosophers saw the *logos* as malicious, John shows that the eternal Word, in whom all things came into being (Jn 1:3), was the source of both "life and light" (Jn 1:4).

The principal distinction between John's use of *logos* and the pagan philosophers' use of the term is seen in Jn 1:14, where he says *ho logos sarx egeneto kai eskenosen en hemin*, "the Word became flesh and put up his tent among us." The pagan philosophers could not have conceived of the *logos* as becoming a human being.

As the Church spread its gospel to the pagans, Jn 1:14 remained the principal stumbling block for many of them. It was a great scandal to hear the words *ho logos sarx egeneto*, "the Word became flesh." To the pagan mind the spiritual realm and the material realm were inseparably divided and incapable of being harmonized. John's theology of the *logos*, on the other hand, teaches precisely that the divine has completely penetrated into the earthly, and that the two are now inseparably joined together for good and love.

Martur—Witness

(Mar'-tour)

Key Passage: Revelation 17:6

Literal Greek: *. . . kai eidon ten gunaika methuousan ek tou haimatos ton hagion kai ek tou haimatos ton marturon Iesou.* (And I saw the woman being drunk from the blood of the holy ones and from the blood of the *witnesses* of Jesus.)

NAB: I saw that the woman was drunk with the blood of God's holy ones and the blood of those martyred for their faith in Jesus.

JB: I saw that she was drunk, drunk with the blood of the saints, and the blood of the martyrs of Jesus. . . .

NEB: The woman, I saw, was drunk with the blood of God's people and with the blood of those who had borne their testimony to Jesus.

NIV: I saw that the woman was drunk with the blood of the saints, the blood of those who bore testimony to Jesus.

As the key passage suggests, *martur*, although literally meaning "witness," came to be applied by the early Church to those who had given the ultimate witness to Jesus, their own lives. Hence our word "martyr."

The related verb is *martureo*, which means "to be a witness." Jesus speaks of his Father as *marturon peri emou*, "witnessing concerning me" (Jn 5:32). Likewise, Luke records the actions of Paul and Barnabas as *marturounti*, "witnessing" (Acts 14:3) to Jesus in their evangelistic ministry. One of the principal teachings of the early Christian *kerygma* (see page 49) was that the Old Testament prophets served to *marturousin* ("witness") to Jesus centuries before his coming (see Acts 10:43).

Just as the Father gave witness to Jesus through the mighty works that Jesus did, and just as the apostles continued to witness to Jesus, so too all Christians are called to be *marturon Iesou*, "witnesses of Jesus."

Meno—Remain, Abide

(Me´-noh)

Key Passage: 1 John 4:15

Literal Greek: ...*hos ean omologese hoti Iesous estin ho huios tou Theou, ho Theos en auto menoi kai autos en to Theo.* (Whoever confesses that Jesus is the Son of God, God in him *remains* and he in God.)

NAB: When anyone acknowledges that Jesus is the Son of God,
God dwells in him
and he in God.

JB: ...God lives in him, and he in God.

NED: ...God dwells in him and he dwells in God.

NIV: ...God lives in him and he in God.

The verb *meno* is used in several places in the New Testament in the form we see in this passage, as well as in other forms. For example, John the Baptist observed that the Spirit came down from heaven and *emeinen* ("remained") on Jesus (Jn 1:32).

A variation of the word is *epimeno*, which means "to continue," as seen in 1 Tm 4:16: "Watch yourself and watch your teaching; *epimene* ['continue in' or 'persevere at'] both tasks." The word *hupomeno* is also related to *meno* and is used in the sense of "endure" or "suffer"; in Heb 12:2, Jesus is said to have "endured" *(hupemeinen)* the cross. And in Jas 1:12, the author says *makarios aner hos hupomenei peirasmon,* "blessed the man who endures trial." Still another variation of the word is *prosmeno,* as seen in Acts 11:23, where Barnabas exhorts the new Christians in Antioch "to remain with *(prosmenein)* the Lord."

Mesites—Mediator

(Mess-it'-ays)

Key Passage: 1 Timothy 2:5

Literal Greek: *Eis gar Theos, eis kai mesites Theou kai anthropon, anthropos Christos Iesous...* (For one is God, one also is the *mediator* of God and man, a man Christ Jesus....)

NAB: "God is one.
One also is the mediator between God and man,
the man Christ Jesus...."

JB: For there is only one God, and there is only one mediator between God and mankind, himself a man, Christ Jesus....

NEB: For there is one God, and also one mediator between God and men, Christ Jesus, himself man....

NIV: For there is one God and one mediator between God and men, the man Christ Jesus....

Mesites is apparently derived from *mesos,* "middle," and

eimi, "to go." Thus *mesites* connotes one who "goes into the middle" or "goes between for someone." The principal New Testament significance of *mesites* is that Jesus Christ is the one who "goes between" humanity and God. The author of Hebrews refers to Christ as *diathekes kaines mesites, "mediator* of a new covenant" (9:15). Jesus is the one who in a sense negotiated a new covenant with God, the old covenant having been abrogated by humanity's sins. The new covenant is a covenant of love and mercy, in which God forgives human sin because of Jesus' sacrifice on the cross.

Metanoeo—Repent

(Met-ah-no-eh´-oh)

Key Passage: Acts 2:38

Literal Greek: "...*metanoesate, kai baptistheto hekastos humon epi to onomati Iesou Christou....*" ("*Repent,* and let each one of yourselves be baptized in the name of Jesus Christ....")

NAB: Peter answered: "You must reform and be baptized, each one of you, in the name of Jesus Christ, that your sins may be forgiven...."

JB: "You must repent," Peter answered, "and every one of you must be baptized in the name of Jesus Christ...."

NEB: "Repent," said Peter, "repent and be baptized, every one of you, in the name of Jesus the Messiah...."

NIV: Peter replied: "Repent and be baptized, every one of you, in the name of Jesus Christ so that your sins may be forgiven."

The verb *metanoeo* comes from *noeo*, "to perceive," and *meta*, "after," and thus means "to perceive afterwards." Its principal connotation is to see things in a different light after having changed one's mind. Paul, for example, feared that his Corinthian flock were not *metanoesanton*, "repenting" (2 Cor 12:21) of their earlier lives of sexual promiscuity. He feared that they had not come to perceive their sexual conduct in a different light, and thus had not changed their mind on the manner in which they behaved.

This sense of *metanoeo* is not similar to "a firm purpose of amendment," but an actual changing of perception and consciousness so that one literally sees things differently and thus now understands former modes of behavior in a different light. As a result, a person is actually able to make a life-changing decision to act in accordance with the new perception of reality.

This is seen in the corresponding noun *metanoia* ("repentance"), as in Heb 12:17 where the author refers to the story of Esau, who sold his birthright and later wanted to change his situation. Yet Esau could not extricate himself from his predicament because he was unable first to experience a *metanoias*, a true change of perception, so that his actions would be in accord with a new mode of under-standing. The NAB translates Esau's predicament by saying that he had "no opportunity to alter his choice." This is a rather limp translation of the original. The JB comes much closer: "He was unable to elicit a change of heart." The latter more correctly emphasizes the essence of *metanoia*— namely, a radical change of perception or consciousness from which a change in behavior spontaneously follows. The New Testament constantly reiterates that a change of heart is prior to a change in life-style. As Paul stated it, "Be transformed by the renewal of your mind" (Rom 12:2).

Monogenes—Only Begotten

(Mon-ah-gen-ays')

Key Passage: John 3:16

Literal Greek: *Houtos gar egapesen ho Theos ton kosmon, hoste ton huion ton monogene edoken....* (For thus loved God the world, so as the Son the *only begotten* he gave....)

NAB: Yes, God so loved the world
that he gave his only Son,
that whoever believes in him may not die
but may have eternal life.

JB: Yes, God loved the world so much that he gave his only Son....

NEB: God loved the world so much that he gave his only Son....

NIV: For God so loved the world that he gave his one and only Son....

It is interesting that none of the modern versions in their rendering of this passage translates *monogenes* as "only begotten." The KJV does capture the full sense of the word, rendering the verse "...his only begotten Son...." Although the new versions correctly emphasize that Jesus is God's only Son, by not fully translating *monogenes* they tend to ignore an important aspect of the eternal Word's nature—that he is the entire representation of the Father's being or, as the author of Hebrews puts it, *charakter tes hupostaseos*, "the representation of the reality" of the Father (Heb 1:3).

The unique connotation of *monogenes* is that the Son is neither created by nor engendered from the Father, but rather shares divinity with the Father in a very unique way. This is not necessarily implied by saying simply that the Word is the "only Son" of the Father. *Monogenes* connotes a lack of beginning in time, a sense of uncreatedness, as in

99

John's opening verse, where he says *en arche en ho logos*, "In the beginning was the Word" (Jn 1:1). That is, the Son never *became* the Son, but always was and is the Son. It is all of this which *monogenes* connotes.

Musterion—Mystery

(Moo-stay'-ree-awn)

Key Passage: Ephesians 1:9

Literal Greek: ...*gnorisas hemin to musterion tou thelematos autou*... (...making known to us the *mystery* of his will....)

NAB: God has given us the wisdom to understand fully the mystery, the plan he was pleased to decree in Christ....

JB: He has let us know the mystery of his purpose, the hidden plan he so kindly made in Christ from the beginning....

NEB: He has made known to us his hidden purpose—such was his will and pleasure determined beforehand in Christ....

NIV: And he made known to us the mystery of his will according to his good pleasure, which he purposed in Christ....

The truths of salvation are essentially *musterion*, that is, they are beyond human understanding. These truths were hidden in God's purpose for all eternity and can be known by humanity only through God's revelation. It was to reveal this *musterion* to humanity that the evangelists were called by God to spread the gospel.

Yet Christianity is a religion not of secret mysteries, but

of love. That is why Paul says that even if *eido ta musteria panta*, "I know all the mysteries" but do not have love, *outhen eimi*, "I am nothing" (1 Cor 13:2). At the time Paul wrote there were various "mystery religions" prevalent in the communities where he preached. The essential element of these religions was their belief in spiritual enlightenment through possession of mysteries revealed only to the chosen.

The Christian understanding of *musterion* is not the same as that of the mystery religions. The connotation of *musterion* in the Christian sense is that one cannot comprehend through human cognition God's loving plan to save humanity, but can only appreciate God's action in history by coming to know Jesus Christ as Savior.

Nomos—Law

(Naw'-maws)

Key Passage: Romans 10:4

Literal Greek: *Telos gar nomou Christos....* (For the end of the *law* Christ is.)

NAB: Christ is the end of the law.

JB: ...now the Law has come to an end with Christ....

NEB: For Christ ends the law....

NIV: Christ is the end of the law....

The New Testament uses *nomos* in various contexts. It can mean simply "law" in the sense of a general principle, as in Rom 3:27 where Paul says that boasting is ruled out through *nomou pisteos*, "the law [or principle] of faith."

Another connotation of *nomos* is the Law of Moses. This usage is intended by Jesus in Mt 5:18 where he says neither one *iota* (the Greek letter "i") nor one *keraia* ("point") *parelthe apo tou nomou*, "shall pass away from the law" until the coming of his Reign in its full power. John likewise refers to this sense in Jn 1:17, where he says the *nomos* was given *dia Mouseos*, "through Moses." Paul writes that the Mosaic law was given by God "in order to increase offenses" (Rom 5:20). In other words, Paul is saying, without the Law of Moses humanity would not have been able to understand what sin was.

One of Paul's principal teachings was that Christians are not justified by *ergon nomou*, "works of law," but rather they are justified *ek pisteos*, "by faith" (Gal 2:16). Having been an ardent follower of the Law himself, Paul wanted his readers to understand that keeping the Law led one not to freedom but to bondage. Only through faith in Jesus Christ does one become free, Paul thought, and this faith is a gift of God's grace.

The first five books of the Hebrew Bible were commonly referred to as "the Law," as in Rom 3:21, where Paul talks about *tou nomou kai ton propheton*, "the law and the prophets." When Paul says that the just person is saved by faith aside from works of the Law, he is not saying that these Old Testament books are invalid. Rather, he is saying that the myriad observances and regulations which the Jews added to God's revealed Law do not lead to righteousness or justice. For Paul *nomos* in the sense of God's revealed Word is much different from these later accretions, which he condemns. Of the revealed "Law" he says *nomos hagios*, "the Law is holy" (Rom 7:12).

Paul uses *nomos* in still another sense. He refers to the *nomon en tois melesin mou*, "law in my members" or the law of his bodily appetites. *Nomos* in this sense is more akin to *sarx* (see p. 122); this law at work in his bodily appetites wars against *to nomo tou noos mou*, "the law of my mind"—the desire to do good. Lacking the power to accomplish what the law of his mind seeks to do, Paul finds himself a prisoner of *to nomo tes hamartias*, the law of sin in his body (Rom 7:23).

Paul plays on the various meanings of *law* in order to

emphasize that salvation is strictly a gift of God's grace. There is nothing one can do without God's aid to free oneself from the tendency toward sin and death which is the natural human conditon.

Onoma—Name

(Ah'-nah-mah)

Key Passage: Philippians 2:10

Literal Greek: . . . *hina en to onomati Iesou pan gonu kumpse epouranion kai epigeion kai katach-thonion*. . . (. . . in order that in the *name* of Jesus every knee should bend, of heavenly beings and earthly beings and beings under the earth. . .)

NAB: . . . So that at Jesus' name
   every knee must bend
   in the heaven, on the earth,
   and under the earth. . . .

JB: . . . So that all beings,
   in the heavens,
   on earth and in the underworld,
   should bend the knee at the name of Jesus.

NEB: . . . that at the name of Jesus every knee
   should bow—in heaven, on earth, and in
   the depths. . . .

NIV: . . . that at the name of Jesus every knee
      should bow,
   in heaven and on earth and under the
      earth. . . .

In ancient times someone's name was not only a means of

103

identification, it served also as a means of expressing the person's character and authority. For this reason Jesus taught his disciples to pray *agiastheto to onoma sou*, "let your name be hallowed" (Mt 6:9). In Luke's Gospel Mary proclaims that *hagion to onoma* ("holy [is] the name") of God (1:49).

In Matthew Jesus says that anyone receiving a little child *epi to onomati mou*, "in my name," *eme dechetai*, "receives me" (Mt 18:5). It was in the name of Jesus, i.e., on the *authority* of Jesus, that the apostles healed the lame and the crippled, as in Acts 3:6. Such actions brought upon the apostles the injunction of the religious establishment not to teach or speak *epi to onomati tou Iesou*, "on the name of Jesus" (Acts 4:18).

The writer of 1 Pt consoled his readers in the face of the insults which they bore *en onomati Christou*, "in the name of Christ" (4:14). The early Christians became identified with the name, i.e., the person and authority of Jesus. Because Jesus' name stood for his authority, the Christians' reliance on his name brought condemnation from the authorities. Further, by sharing Jesus' name the Christians opened themselves to the persecution and rejection which Jesus himself had experienced. Yet the early evangelists undertook their mission precisely because they knew that, by believing in Jesus, people could have *zoen en to onomati autou*, "life in his name" (Jn 20:31).

Ouranos—Heaven

(Oo-rah-naws')

Key Passage: Revelation 21:1

Literal Greek: *Kai eidon ouranon kainon kai gen kainen ho gar protos ouranos kai he prote ge apelthan....* (I saw a new *heaven* and new earth; for the first *heaven* and the first earth passed away....)

NAB: Then I saw new heavens and a new earth. The former heavens and the former earth had passed away....

JB: Then I saw a new heaven and a new earth; the first heaven and the first earth had disappeared now....

NEB: Then I saw a new heaven and a new earth, for the first heaven and the first earth had vanished....

NIV: Then I saw a new heaven and a new earth, for the first heaven and the first earth had passed away....

Ouranos is used in the New Testament principally to denote God's eternal home, as in the key passage. It has, however, several related meanings. For example, Jesus in Mt 6:26 exhorts his audience to look at the birds *tou ouranou*, "of heaven," usually translated "of the air."

The theological significance of *ouranos* stems from the fact that the incarnate Word came from "heaven" to become a man. Jesus is *ho ek tou ouranou*, "the one out of heaven" (Jn 3:13). Having completed his salvific ministry, Jesus has now returned to heaven. He *estin en dezia Theou, poreutheis eis ouranon*, "is at the right hand of God, having gone into heaven..." (1 Pt 3:22).

The apostles witnessed Jesus' ascension into heaven in

Lk 24:51, although there the word *ouranos* is not used. Rather the Greek simply says *dieste ap' auton*, "he withdrew from them." In Luke's second volume, he likewise omits *ouranos*, saying simply that Jesus *anelemphthe*, "was taken up" (Acts 1:2). The NAB's addition of the words "to heaven" is an interpretation rather than a translation, but does convey the sense of the Greek.

Once Jesus ascended to heaven, then the Holy Spirit was *apostalenti ap' ouranou*, "sent forth from heaven" (1 Pt 1:12) to empower the disciples to carry on Jesus' ministry of building up the Kingdom.

Finally, heaven is to be the eternal home of the elect: "We have a house *aionion en tois ouranois*, eternal in the heavens" (2 Cor 5:1). At the *parousia* (see p. 107), Jesus will come again on the clouds *tou ouranou* ("of heaven") "with much power and glory" (Mt 24:30).

Ouranos is to be contrasted with *geenna*, "hell," which Mark defines as *to pur to asbeston*, "the unquenchable fire" (9:44). Matthew speaks of *geenna* as a place where "both soul and body" shall be destroyed (10:28).

Parousia—Coming

(Pair-oo-seé-ah)

Key Passage: Matthew 24:3b

Literal Greek: "...ti to semeion tes ses parousias kai sunteleias tou aionos?" ("What will be the sign of your presence and of the completion of the age?")

NAB: "What will be the sign of your coming and the end of the world?"

JB: "...what will be the sign of your coming and of the end of the world?"

NEB: "And what will be the signal of your coming and the end of the age?"

NIV: "...what will be the sign of your coming and of the end of the age?"

As indicated above, *parousia* can mean both "coming" and "presence." Literally the word means *para* ("with") *ousia* ("being"), "being with." It thus suggests both an arrival and a continual staying with someone.

Paul reminds his readers how they obeyed him in his *apousia* ("absence") as much as in his *parousia* ("presence") (Phil 2:12). The early Church associated *parousia* with Jesus' Transfiguration, as in 2 Pt 1:16 where the author refers to his eyewitness of Jesus' *parousian* (translated "majesty" in the NAB, 1:17).

The principal usage of the word by the early Church was to connote the *Second* Coming. Paul refers to Jesus' *parousia* in 1 Cor 15:23, and in 1 Thes 4:15 says that those who survive until Jesus' *parousian* "will in no way have an advantage over those who have fallen asleep," i.e., those who have died before the *parousia*. Matthew describes the suddenness with which the *parousia* will occur (Mt 24:27). (See p. 17 for analysis of another word used to refer to

Jesus' Second Coming: *apokalupsin*, or "revelation.")

Pater—Father

(Pah-tayr')

Key Passage: Matthew 5:48

Literal Greek: *"Esesthe oun humeis teleioi hos ho pater humon ho ouranious teleios estin."* ("Therefore be perfect as your heavenly *Father* is perfect.")

NAB: "In a word, you must be made perfect as your heavenly Father is perfect."

JB: "You must therefore be perfect just as your heavenly Father is perfect."

NEB: "There must be no limit to your goodness, as your heavenly Father's goodness knows no bounds."

NIV: "Be perfect, therefore, as your heavenly Father is perfect."

Pater has several connotations in the New Testament, including simply the biological father of a family. In Mt 3:9 it is used of Abraham to show that he is the "founding father" of a people.

The word can also refer to Christian elders, as in 1 Jn 2:13, where the author says *grapho humin, pateres*, "I write to you, fathers." The early Church used "father" to refer to its elders or teachers as spiritual fathers. Paul reminds his beloved Corinthians that for their sake he *egennesa* ("begat") them (1 Cor 4:15).

This custom was not disobedience to the Lord's commandment, *kai patera me kalesete humon epi tes ges*, "and

do not call [someone] your father on earth" (Mt 23:9). This
verse does not proscribe the use of the word *father*, but
exhorts Christians not to lord it over one another as the
rabbis and masters of the Law did in Jesus' day.

The primary theological significance of *pater* resides in
the concept of God's "fatherhood." Jn 1:12-13 says that
we have been given *exousian* (the "right" or "power," see
p. 51) to be called children of God. And in Eph 2:18 the
writer teaches that, through Christ, the believer has *prosa-
gogne* ("access" or "approach") to the Father. That is why
Christians are to be perfect as the Father is perfect: Having
been given the authority of children they must now imitate
their Father.

Petra   Rock

(Pet'-rah)

Key Passage: Matthew 16:18

Literal Greek: "... *kai epi taute te petra oikodomeso mou
ten ekklesian....*" ("...and on this *rock*
I will build of me the Church.")

NAB: "I for my part declare to you, you are
'Rock,' and on this rock I will build my
church, and the jaws of death shall not
prevail against it."

JB: "So I now say to you: You are Peter and
on this rock I will build my Church."

NEB: "And I say this to you: You are Peter, the
Rock; and on this rock I will build my
church...."

NIV: "And I tell you that you are Peter, and on
this rock I will build my church...."

A consideration of *petra* is helpful today perhaps solely for the reason that some fundamentalist groups have come up with the rather bizarre interpretation of this verse to mean that Jesus said, "Peter, you are a pebble," or (even more absurdly), "a chip off the old rock." In actuality, *petra* does not mean "pebble" or "chip," but a huge mass of rock, such as the Rock of Gibraltar. The Greek word for stone in the sense of something movable is *petros*, not *petra*. (Note also that the Greek word for pebble is *psephos*, and the Greek word for stone is *lithos*.)

The significance of *petra* is highlighted in Lk 6:48 in the parable of the man who builds his house on rock (*petran*), a solid foundation of immovable substrata. In the same way, Christ is saying that he intends to build his Church on a stable foundation—namely, on Peter.

By playing on the words *petros* (the nickname given to Simon the apostle) and *petra*, Jesus is reminding Peter that in himself he is movable, but through his faith in Jesus as the Son of God he is an immovable foundation. It is this faith in Jesus which is the sure and certain rock of the Church. In this sense, not only is the apostle Peter "rock," but likewise all Christians who follow Peter by proclaiming faith in Jesus are the Church's foundation.

Phos—Light

(Fohs [rhymes with close])

Key Passage: John 1:5

Literal Greek: *Kai to phos en te skotia phainei, kai he skotia auto ou katelaben.* (And the *light* in the darkness shines, and the darkness it does not overtake.)

NAB: The light shines on in darkness,
        a darkness that did not overcome it.

JB: ...a light that shines in the dark,
        a light that darkness could not overpower.

NEB: The light shines on in the dark, and the darkness has never mastered it.

NIV: The light shines in the darkness, but the darkness has not understood it.

Just as God is life, so also he is light. And just as those who share God's life are raised to a new state of existence, so also do they become *huious tou photos,* "sons of the light" (Lk 16:8).

In its theological sense, *light* in the New Testament means the absolute truth and knowledge which is the very nature of God, as opposed to the darkness of ignorance and illusion which is the lot of humanity.

John in particular dwells on Jesus' role as light and light-giver. He says that *to phos eleluthen eis ton kosmon,* "the light has come into the world..." (Jn 3:19). Elsewhere, Jesus says of himself *ego eimi to phos tou kosmou,* "I am the light of the world" (Jn 8:12). John makes it clear that it is Jesus who gives light to humanity, and that without Jesus' illumination humanity is bound to a life of darkness. So Jesus tells his disciples to walk *hos to phos echete,* "while you have the light" (Jn 12:35).

The early Church reiterated this understanding of Jesus

111

when the first evangelists equated Jesus with the *phos ethnon* ("light of the nations") referred to in Isaiah 49:6 (Acts 13:47).

There are several related verbs, such as *photizo* which means "to give light to." Eternal life with God is described as constant light and the absence of all darkness; the elect will no longer have need of sunlight because God himself *photisei ep autous*, "will shed light on them" (Rev 22:5).

In Luke 11:33-36, Jesus uses the parable of the lamp hidden under a bowl and the metaphor of the eye and the lamp to teach that the believer is called to banish the illusion of spiritual darkness. In Lk 11:36 Jesus compares this enlightenment process to the action of a lamp which *photize se*, "enlightens you." The source of Christian enlightenment is Jesus himself, *to phos to alethinon ho photizei panta anthropon*, "the true light which enlightens every man" (Jn 1:9).

Thus, Christians are called to a state of enlightenment, or higher spiritual consciousness, in which they themselves know the truths of God. The writer of Ephesians refers to this when he prays that *pephotismenous*, "having been enlightened," we may come to know fully "the wealth of his glorious heritage" (Eph 1:18). The same author says that his own ministry has been *photisai*, "to bring to light" the mysteries of God which had been hidden for ages (Eph 3:9).

Pistis—Belief, Faith

(Piss'-tiss)

Key Passage: Romans 10:17

Literal Greek: ...*pistis ex akoes he de akoe dia rhematos Christou.* (*Faith* is from hearing, and the hearing through a word of Christ.)

NAB: Faith, then, comes through hearing, and what is heard is the word of Christ.

JB: So faith comes from what is preached, and what is preached comes from the word of Christ.

NEB: We conclude that faith is awakened by the message, and the message that awakens it comes through the word of Christ.

NIV: Consequently, faith comes from hearing the message, and the message is heard through the word of Christ.

Pistis is derived from *pisteou*, "to believe," and is also related to *peitho*, "to persuade."

Pistis has several connotations in the New Testament. It has the sense of "trust" as in 1 Cor 2:5, where Paul reminds the Corinthians that their *pistis* is durable because it is based on the power of God. In Gal 5:22 *pistis* connotes "faithfulness," rather than one's initial belief in Jesus as Lord. In Acts 6:7 the word is used to designate the *content* of the beliefs which were shared by the early Christians: "There were many Jewish priests among those who embraced *te pistei,* the faith."

Pistis is not just a decision to believe that someone's word is reliable. Rather, *pistis* suggests a life-changing conviction which manifests itself in proclaiming God as the source of truth. Thus the concept of faith includes not only "belief," but also the change in conduct which is inspired

113

by surrender to God's purpose. The New Testament does not distinguish between faith and works as two *separate aspects* of the Christian life.

The definition of faith in Heb 11:1 is perhaps one of the most disputed translations in the New Testament: *Estin de pistis elpizomenon hupostasis, pragmaton elegchos ou blepomenon.* (Literally, "Now faith is the reality of things being hoped for and the proof of things not being seen.")

The NAB translates the verse, "Faith is confident assurance concerning what we hope for, and conviction about things we do not see." The JB has, "Only faith can guarantee the blessings that we hope for, or prove the existence of the realities that at present remain unseen." The NEB says, "Faith gives substance to our hopes, and makes us certain of realities we do not see." Finally, the NIV reads, "Now faith is being sure of what we hope for and certain of what we do not see."

The problems which arise over the translation of the verse concern the meaning of the word *hupostasis*. The word can mean "reality" or "substance" as well as "assurance," as the NAB has it. *Reality* gives faith more of an objective cast; if *assurance* is used, then faith becomes more subjective.

From the context of the following verses, it appears that the author leans more towards the subjective interpretation of faith given by the NAB translation. In this passage, faith is not so much the acceptance of God's truths as it is perseverance in the acceptance already made. In the examples which the author gives (see 11:1-40) faith is presented as a disposition or mental attitude exercised by the believer, and thus becomes more akin to fidelity or trust.

This interpretation would be consistent with Jesus' words in Mt 17:20-21, where he chides his disciples for being unable to rebuke a demon. The reason Jesus gives for the disciples' lack of power is *dia ten oligopistian humon*, "because of your little faith." Obviously, Jesus here is not referring to faith in the sense of surrendering one's life to the truth of God as embodied in Jesus' person. In this passage, as in Hebrews, faith once again is seen as a subjective attitude.

Perhaps the best way to distinguish between the two major connotations of faith is to discuss *pistis* under two different headings: "Faith 1" and "Faith 2."

"Faith 1" is the faith necessary for salvation. Paul devoted a good deal of his writings to a discussion of this faith. Coming out of a legalistic, institutionalized religious background, Paul wanted his readers to understand that human-made religiosity (what Paul called "works of the law") could not bring one to salvation. Only "Faith 1" could do this.

For example, Paul scolded the Galatian Christians for losing sight of the primacy of faith in their lives and for slipping back into a reliance on works as the key element in their relationship with God. Paul asked them, "Is it because you observe the law or because you have faith in what you heard that God lavishes the Spirit on you and works wonders in your midst?" (Gal 3:3). In the same letter he wrote, "Each one of you is a son of God because of your faith in Jesus Christ" (Gal 3:26).

"Faith 2," on the other hand, is the attitudinal disposition which Christians need in order to make the gospel real in their lives. An example of the New Testament's usage of this faith appears in Jesus' words, "I assure you if you had faith the size of a mustard seed, you would be able to say to this mountain, 'Move from here to there,' and it would move. Nothing would be impossible for you" (Mt 17:20).

Jesus, of course, is not saying, "Unless your faith is strong enough to move a mountain, you are not saved." He is instead talking about an attitude of trust ("Faith 2") which those who already have been given "Faith 1" should exercise.

Thus, the New Testament uses *pistis* both in the sense of the initial life-changing decision to accept Jesus Christ, and also in the sense of a continuing attitude of trust in God's power in one's daily life as a Christian.

Ploutos—Riches, Wealth

(Ploo'-taws)

Key Passage: Matthew 13:22

Literal Greek: ...*he merimna tou aionos kai he apate tou ploutou sumpnigei ton logon....* (...the anxiety of the age and the deceit of *riches* choke the word....)

NAB: What was sown among briers is the man who hears the message, but then worldly anxiety and the lure of money choke it off.

JB: ...But the worries of this world and the lure of riches choke the word and so he produces nothing.

NEB: ...but worldly cares and the false glamour of wealth choke it, and it proves barren.

NIV: ...but the worries of this life and the deceitfulness of wealth choke it, making it unfruitful.

The NIV does the best job of translating this passage. It emphasizes that the New Testament finds in *ploutos* ("riches") an element of deceit or illusion. It is this element which makes riches so incompatible with true spiritual existence.

Ploutos gives us the false sense of security that we've "made it," that we can ignore God and base our lives on our own accomplishments. We become like the *plousion* ("rich man") in Lk 12:16 who tore down his grain bins to build bigger ones. If we live in an illusory state we are *aphron* ("a fool," Lk 12:20), literally, one who is deceived or tricked by another.

The New Testament contrasts earthly *ploutos* with God's riches. Paul refers to *ploutou tes chrestotetos* ("riches of the kindness") of God (Rom 2:4). Likewise, he praises *bathos ploutou kai sophias kai gnoseos Theou*, "the depth of the

116

riches and of the wisdom and of the knowledge of God"
(Rom 11:33).

A related word is *plousios*, "the rich," and it is in the
use of this word that we find the New Testament's ultimate
evaluation of *ploutos*. In Lk 6:24 Jesus unequivocally says
ouai humin tois plousiois, "Woe to you, the rich ones." No
matter how much we wish those words would disappear, the
Greek leaves little room for either comfort or compromise.

Pneuma Hagion—Holy Spirit

(Puh-noo'-mah Hah'-gee-on)

Key Passage: Acts 19:2

Literal Greek: "....*ei pneuma hagion elabete pisteusuntes?*"
                 ("...if upon believing you received the
                 Holy Spirit ?")

NAB: "Did you receive the Holy Spirit when you
                 became believers?"

JB,NEB,NIV: Virtually identical to NAB.

The same word *pneuma* is used for the human spirit (see
page 83) and for the Holy Spirit of God (in older translations
known as the "Holy Ghost"). In the days when the New
Testament was being composed, the early Church had not
fully developed its theology of the Holy Spirit, and thus
there is a good deal of ambiguity in the usage of *pneuma
hagion*.

Jesus himself introduced the notion of the Third Person
of the Trinity to his disciples. In Matthew 22:43 he refers
to David's having spoken *en pneumati*, "in the Spirit." In
John's Gospel, Jesus' teaching becomes much clearer. For
example, Jesus tells his disciples that the Father will send *to
pneuma to hagion*, "the Holy Spirit" *en to onomati mou*, "in

117

my name." This Spirit "will instruct you in everything, and remind you of all that I told you" (Jn 14:26).

Paul refers to the Holy Spirit as *pneuma Theou*, "the Spirit of God" (Rom 8:9), *pneumati Theou zontos*, "the spirit of a living God" (2 Cor 3:3), *pneuma Christou*, "Spirit of Christ" (Rom 8:9), and *pneuma tou huiou*, "the Spirit of the Son" (Gal 4:6). Paul was groping for an adequate way to express his understanding of the Holy Spirit as a distinct divine Person.

Despite the New Testament writers' struggle to make their understanding of the Holy Spirit more concrete, it is nonetheless obvious that they are referring to what we today know as the Third Person of the Trinity. This is obvious in such verses as John 7:39, where the writer refers to *tou pneumatos*, "the Spirit" whom those who came to believe in Jesus were to receive after Jesus had been glorified.

As the later New Testament writers reflected on the earlier revelation of God's work through the Holy Spirit, they became more confident in referring to the Spirit in terms of a distinct Person in the Trinity, with a distinct purpose and mission among humanity. See, for example, Eph 1:13 where the writer reminds his readers that when they came to believe in Christ they were "sealed *to pneumati...to hagio*, with the Holy Spirit who had been promised."

Interestingly, *pneuma* is neuter in Greek, and yet in several places the New Testament writers use the masculine pronoun *ekeinos* ("he") to refer to the Holy Spirit. For instance, Jn 15:26 says of the Spirit, "He will bear witness on my behalf." In all probability the word which Jesus himself actually used when speaking his native Aramaic was *rûchâ*, which is a feminine noun. Of course, the Holy Spirit is neither male nor female (nor neuter), but something beyond our entire concept of gender. Nonetheless, it would be just as accurate to refer to the Spirit as "she" in some New Testament passages as "he" or "it."

Proseuchomai—To Pray

(Praws-you'-ko-my)

Key Passage: Ephesians 6:18

Literal Greek: ...*dia pases proseuches kai deeseos, proseuchomenoi en panti kairo en pneumati...* (...by means of all *prayer* and petition, *praying* at every time in spirit.)

NAB: At every opportunity pray in the Spirit, using prayers and petitions of every sort.

JB: Pray all the time, asking for what you need, praying in the Spirit on every possible occasion.

NEB: Give yourselves wholly to prayer and entreaty; pray on every occasion in the power of the Spirit.

NIV: And pray in the Spirit on all occasions with all kinds of prayers and requests.

Proseuchomai (note the resemblance to the English "prosecute") is the most frequent word for "pray" in the New Testament. The remainder of the verse, "Pray constantly and attentively for all in the holy company" (6:18b, NAB), suggests the usual connotation of *proseuchomai*—namely, interceding, petitioning, or intervening on someone's behalf.

A related word is *euchomai,* as in 2 Cor 13:7, where Paul says *euchometha,* "we pray to God." Paul is expressing his ardent desire or wish that the Corinthians would heed his advice. Notice that *euchomai* is simply *proseuchomai* without the *pros.* The Greek preposition *pro* means "before" or "in front of," and thus *proseuchomai* may be thought of as more formal, even *liturgical* prayer. In the key passage the Spirit intercedes for us *before* God's very throne, i.e., the Spirit formally prays to the Father on our behalf.

Perhaps one of the most inscrutable commandments of

119

the entire New Testament is that of 1 Thes 5:17, where Paul urges his readers to *adialeiptos proseuchesthe*, "unceasingly pray." For this to be possible, prayer obviously must be something other than verbal petition. It must be a deeper mental process, an awareness of God so pervasive that prayer becomes a permanent feature of one's consciousness.

Rhema—Word

(Ray'-mah)

Key Passage: Ephesians 6:17

Literal Greek: . . . *kai ten perikephalaian tou soteriou dexasthe, kai ten machairan tou pneumatos, ho estin rhema Theou*. . . . (And the helmet of salvation take, and the sword of the spirit, which is the *word* of God. . . .)

NAB: Take the helmet of salvation and the sword of the spirit, the word of God.

JB: And then you must accept salvation from God to be your helmet and receive the word of God from the Spirit to use as a sword.

NEB: Take salvation for helmet; for sword, take that which the Spirit gives you—the words that come from God.

NIV: Take the helmet of salvation and the sword of the Spirit, which is the word of God.

Some understanding of *logos* (see p. 91) will yield a better understanding of *rhema*. The latter refers more specifically to the *spoken* word, as in Mt 12:36, where Jesus says that on judgment day we will have to account for every *rhema argon* ("idle word") which we have spoken. We see the distinction between *logos* and *rhema* also in Jn 3:34, where the writer says, "the one whom God has sent *(logos)* speaks *ta rhemata* ("the words") of God." *Logos* thus refers to the eternal Word, while *rhema* refers to the revealed, oral words which the Son of God speaks to humanity.

Rhema also refers to Scripture, as in Rom 10:8 where Paul (quoting Dt 30:14) says that "the word *(to rhema)* is near you, on your lips, and in your heart." He identifies this *rhema* with the gospel when he equates it with "the word of faith which we preach" (Rom 10:8). This is what the writer means when he says to take on "the word of God" (Eph 6:17): to study and learn the Scriptures in order to be able to use them in one's daily life to combat evil and injustice.

Perhaps one of the best illustrations of this thought in later Christian tradition is the commandment which St. Benedict gave to his monks. They were to "chew the word" while they performed their daily manual labor—to meditate constantly on a particular passage from Scripture while they worked. Following the advice in Eph 6:17, Benedict knew that the words of Scripture were a powerful force for personal holiness and growth in the Lord.

Sarx—Flesh

(Sarx)

Key Passage: Galatians 5:17

Literal Greek: ...*gar sarx epithumei kata tou pneumatos, to de pneuma kata tes sarkos, tauta gar allelois antikeitai.* (...for the *flesh* lusts against the Spirit, and the Spirit against the *flesh*, for each opposes the other.)

NAB: The flesh lusts against the spirit and the spirit against the flesh; the two are directly opposed.

JB: ...self-indulgence is the opposite of Spirit, the Spirit is totally against such a thing....

NEB: That [your lower] nature sets its desires against the Spirit, while the Spirit fights against it.

NIV: For the sinful nature desires what is contrary to the Spirit, and the Spirit what is contrary to the sinful nature.

Sarx is perhaps one of the most misunderstood words in the New Testament. As suggested by the key passage, the theological connotation of *sarx* is the lesser or weaker aspect of human nature which causes humanity to sin. Paul is not saying that human flesh itself is evil or that the sexual appetite is wrong. Instead, he teaches that, left to itself, our human nature will choose the animal appetite rather than spiritual truths.

Sarx is used as a synonym for humanity itself. Mt 24:22 refers to *pasa sarx* ("all flesh") in the sense of the human race. If the word also has this connotation, then flesh is obviously not in itself evil, since *ho logos sarx egeneto*, "the Word *became* flesh" (Jn 1:14).

Sarx is not to be equated with *soma*, "body." In 2 Pt

2:18 the author condemns *epithumiais sarkos*, or "lusts of the flesh." The New Testament does not take a negative view toward the human body; rather, it teaches that there is within *human nature* the tendency toward lust, selfishness, degradation, etc.

Sarx is really an attitude or a perspective on life which is natural to humanity and which can be elevated toward truth and goodness only by the redeeming power of the indwelling Holy Spirit. Paul refers to this change of perspective in his own life when he says that now, after being remade by the Holy Spirit, "we know no man *kata sarka* (according to the flesh)" (2 Cor 5:16).

Paul then goes on to define the opposite condition from *sarx*, where he says if anyone is in Christ he is *kaine ktisis*, "a new creation" (2 Cor 5:17). For Paul, *ta archaia*, "the old things"—including the perspective of *sarx*—*parelthen*, *idou gegonen kaina*, "have passed away, and behold, have become new."

Thus in Christianity the human body is another aspect of God's good creation. Left to its own devices the body will be motivated by *sarx*, and thus choose evil instead of good. Once the body surrenders to the power of the Spirit, however, it becomes part of the new creation which Paul talks about, leaving *sarx* behind. *Sarx* is thus not something which dies only when the body dies, but rather it dies gradually as the life of the Spirit replaces it and transforms it into the new creation.

Soteria—Salvation

(So-tay-ree-ah)

Key Passage: Romans 13:11

Literal Greek: ...*nun gar egguteron hemon he soteria he hote episteusamen.* (...for now nearer is our *salvation* than when we believed.)

NAB: It is now the hour for you to wake from sleep, for our salvation is closer than when we first accepted the faith.

JB: ...our salvation is even nearer than it was when we were converted.

NEB: ...for deliverance is nearer to us now than it was when first we believed.

NIV: ...because our salvation is nearer now than when we first believed.

Of the four translations above, the JB comes nearest to approximating the sense of the Greek. It suggests that *soteria* is the end product of a life lived by a justified and redeemed Christian.

Soteria is not a one-moment phenomenon, as sidewalk evangelists of our day would have us believe when they ask if we "have been saved." As the key passage implies, Paul understood salvation as an ongoing reality coming to fruition only in the Endtime. He expresses this thought elsewhere, telling his readers to *soterian katergazesthe,* "work out salvation" (Phil 2:12).

In other words, Paul writes to believers who have already accepted Jesus Christ as their Lord and Savior, but who nonetheless need to be exhorted to continue living for salvation. Paul sees salvation principally as the end result of "justification" (see page 32), "reconciliation" (see page 84) and "redemption" (see page 19).

Like most Christians of his day Paul, at least in his

124

early period, expected Jesus' *parousia* (see p. 107) to occur within his own lifetime. As he grew older and realized that Jesus was not coming again soon, Paul had to expand his concept of salvation. He did this by shifting the emphasis of salvation from the "now" to the Endtime.

An example of Paul's earlier thinking on the imminence of salvation is seen where he quotes Isaiah 49:8 in 2 Cor 6:2: *idou nun hemera soterias,* "behold now is the day of salvation." The "now-ness" of salvation is likewise seen in the Zacchaeus story (Lk 19:1-10). Jesus says *semeron soteria to oiko touto egeneto,* "today salvation came to this house" (Lk 19:9). Notice that the tense of the verb *egeneto* is in the past, expressing the idea that Zacchaeus has *already been* saved because he repented and put his faith in Jesus.

It seems difficult to reconcile the New Testament's here-and-now perspective on salvation with its Endtime perspective, but there was no conflict in the mind of the New Testament writers. Jesus *is* salvation in his person and in his being. One who accepts Jesus is therefore saved *now,* even though the fruits of salvation are not immediately perceptible.

This does not mean, however, that the New Testament teaches a theology of "once saved, always saved" in the sense that one can never lose or repudiate the gift of salvation. The author of Hebrews makes this point clear: "If we sin willfully after receiving the truth, there remains for us no further sacrifice for sin—only a fearful expectation of judgment in a flaming fire to consume the adversaries of God" (Heb 10:26-27, NAB)

Soteria therefore does not suggest resting on one's laurels after having made an initial life-changing decision to put faith in Jesus Christ. Such a passive understanding of *soteria* is held by certain fundamentalist groups today. For such persons once one is "saved," all that remains in the Christian life is vindication at the final judgment.

Telos—End, Fulfillment

(Teh'-laws)

Key Passage: Luke 22:37b

Literal Greek: *"...kai gar to peri emou telos echei."*
("...for indeed the thing concerning me has an *end."*)

NAB: "All that has to do with me approaches its climax."

JB: "Yes, what scripture says about me is even now reaching its fulfillment."

NEB: "...indeed, all that is written of me is being fulfilled."

NIV: "Yes, what is written about me is reaching its fulfillment."

Telos has various meanings in the New Testament. In 1 Pt 4:7 the author says the *telos* ("end") has drawn near, meaning the end of the earthly era.

Telos also has the connotation of "goal" or "purpose." For example, Paul says that Christ is the *telos nomou*, "end of the Law" (Rom 10:4) in the sense that Christ is the fulfillment of the Law. This is the meaning of *telos* in our key passage, where Jesus refers to his coming passion and death as the fulfillment of Scripture.

Telos is also used in the sense of "ultimately" or "perfectly." In Jn 13:1 the author refers to Jesus' *agapesas tous idious...eis telos*, "loving his own...to the end."

A related word, formed from *telos*, is *suntelia*. It connotes "completion," as where Jesus tells his disciples that he will be with them always, *heos tes sunteleias tou aionos*, "until the completion of the age" (Mt 28:20).

Aionos ("age," from *aion*) brings us to another important New Testament concept related to *telos*: *eschatos*, an adjective meaning "last," and the related noun *eschaton*, the "end" or the "last days." The early Church's thinking on the *eschaton* has led to an entire area of study known as *eschatology*, the study of the last things. *Telos, eschatos* and *aion* are all related in that they all refer to the eternal age which will follow the consummation of the early age in which the Church now exists. The early Christians believed that they were living in the Endtime; Heb 1:2 speaks of the present generation as *eschatou ton hemeron*, "the last days."

Paul gives a good analysis of the difference between earthly time and time of the *aion* in 2 Cor 4:18. What is seen, he says, is *proskaira* ("temporary"), while what is not seen (in the sense of what is awaited) is *aionia* ("eternal"). Eternal life is the life of God himself, which is likewise endless. (See Rom 16:26, where Paul refers to *tou aioniou Theou*, "the eternal God.") In leaving earthly time and passing into the *aion*, Christians terminate temporal existence and enter the timeless existence of God himself.

Thanatos—Death

(Thahn'-ah-taws)

Key Passage: Romans 5:14

Literal Greek: ...*alla ebasileusen ho thanatos apo Adam mechri Mouseos....* (...but *death* reigns from Adam until Moses.)

NAB: ...I say, from Adam to Moses death reigned....

JB: ...yet death reigned over all from Adam to Moses....

NEB: But death held sway from Adam to Moses....

NIV: Nevertheless, death reigned from the time of Adam to the time of Moses....

Thanatos as used in this key passage connotes the radical separation of humanity from God. Death is not seen simply as the cessation of ordinary biological life, but as the *absence* of life apart from God. It is to overcome *thanatos* and to restore humanity to communion with God that Jesus came into the world. In Jn 5:24 Jesus assures those who believe in him that they shall possess eternal life, having *metabebeken ek tou thanatou eis ten zoen,* "passed over out of death into life."

Thanatos (as a theological concept) results not from the natural condition of the universe, but from sin. In destroying sin on the cross, Jesus thus destroyed *thanatos.* He is said to have borne our sins in his body so that *hamartiais apogenomenoi te dikaiosune zesomen,* "dying to sin we might live for righteousness" (1 Pt 2:24). *Apogenomenoi* is a participle of the verb *apoginomai,* which literally means "to be separated from." The writer is telling us that by dying for us Jesus "separated" us from our sins.

In addition to this theological sense, *thanatos* also has

128

the more ordinary sense of biological death. For example, in
Jn 11:13 Jesus speaks of *tou thanatou*, "the death" of
Lazarus—physical death. Of course, as we usually find in
John's Gospel, Lazarus's physical death is at the same time a
sign of the death of sin shared by all people who have not
yet received the saving redemption of Jesus Christ. Thus
Jesus' raising Lazarus from the dead is consistent with the
"theological" understanding of *thanatos* we have discussed
above. In raising Lazarus from *thanatos*, Jesus illustrates that
"ego eimi he anastasis kai he zoe, I am the Resurrection
and the life" (Jn 11:25). Even though Jesus has *resuscitated*
Lazarus (see p. 14), this resuscitation is a *sign* of the
resurrection which Jesus will bring all who believe in him.

Theos—God

(Theh'-aws)

Key Passage: Romans 8:31b

Literal Greek: *Ei ho Theos huper hemon, tis kath hemon?*
(If *God* is on behalf of us, who [is] against
us?)

NAB: If God is for us, who can be against us?

JB: With God on our side who can be against
us?

NEB: If God is on our side, who is against us?

NIV: If God is for us, who can be against us?

Theos, of course, is not a word that Christians invented. It
was the word for the Greeks' own gods, as in Acts 14:11
where the Lycaonians mistakenly confuse Barnabas and Paul
for *hoi Theoi*, "the gods" Zeus and Hermes.

The New Testament leaves little doubt that *Christos*

(Christ) is *Theos* (God). Note the characteristics which the New Testament attributes to *Theos* on the one hand and to Jesus the *Christos* on the other:

Attributes of Theos	Attributes of Christos
...*eis gar Theos*... (For there is one God, 1 Tm 2:5)	...*ho on epi panton*... (The one being over all..., Rom 9:5)
...*hosper gar ho pater echei zoen eauto*... (...for as the Father has life in himself..., Jn 5:26)	"...*ego eimi he hodos kai he aletheia kai he zoe*." ("I am the way and the truth and the life...," Jn 14:6)
...*en to Theo to ta panta ktisanti* (...in God the one having created all things, Eph 3:9)	...*en auto ektisthe ta panta*... (In him were created all things..., Col 1:16)
...*ho Theos phos estin*...(God is light..., 1 Jn 1:5)	"...*ego eimi to phos tou kosmou*..." ("I am the light of world," Jn 8:12)

130

Zoe—Life

(Zo-ay')

Key Passage: John 10:10b

Literal Greek: *"Ego elthon hina zoen echosin kai perisson echosin."* ("I came that *life* they may have and abundantly they may have it.")

NAB: "I came
that they might have life
and have it to the full."

JB, NIV: Virtually identical to NAB.

NEB: "I have come that men may have life, and may have it in all its fullness."

Zoe is used of God's eternal life in the New Testament: "for the Father has *zoen* in himself..." (Jn 5:26). In Jesus this divine *zoe* was *ephanerothe* ("manifested," 1 Jn 1:2), and it is to this *zoen* which the evangelist *marturoumen* ("bears witness," 1 Jn 1:2). The evangelist John, in particular, is absorbed with this idea of presenting Jesus as "new life."

Paul echoes John by presenting human life before Christ as a condition in which *ebasileusen ho thanatos*, "death reigned" (Rom 5:14, see p. 128). Without Christ, then, humanity is alienated or "estranged" (NAB) from *tes zoes tou Theou*, "a life in God" (Eph 4:18); but through faith in Jesus, humanity *eche zoen aionion*, "may have life eternal" (Jn 3:15). Once someone comes to faith in Jesus, he or she is removed from *thanatou*, "death," *eis ten zoen*, "into the life" (1 Jn 3:14).

One day, even our bodies will share in the resurrected life of Jesus, according to Paul: so that what is *thneton* ("mortal") *katapothe* ("may be swallowed up") *hupo tes zoes* ("by the life") (2 Cor 5:4). The author of 2 Tm refers to this life in the resurrected body as *aphtharsian*, "incorruption" or, as the NAB has it, "immortality" (2 Tm 1:10).

131

Zoe differs from other New Testament words for life such as *bios*. *Bios* refers more to ordinary earthly life, as in Lk 8:14 where, in the Parable of the Sower and the Seed, Jesus refers to those who are choked by *hedonon tou biou*, "the pleasures of life." We could say that *zoe* is "vertical life," the timeless life in Jesus, and that *bios* is "horizontal" or chronological life. In essence, what Jesus accomplishes is to transform us from a state of *bios* to a state of *zoe*. This is the implication in the key verse concept of "life to the full" or "abundant life."

A related verb is *zoopoieo*, "to give life to" or "to make alive," a combination of *poieo*, "to make," and *zoe*, "life." In Jn 5:21 the verb is used to refer to the Father's action in raising the dead and giving them life. In the same verse this power of the Father is said to be entrusted also to the Son, so that *kai ho huios hous thelei zoopoiei*, "also the Son makes alive [or gives life to] whom he wills."

In 1 Cor 15:36 Paul compares the Christian's rising from death to life to the action of a seed which dies in the soil and then *zoopoieitai* ("is made alive"). Finally, John teaches that the source of new life is the Spirit: *to pneuma estin to zoopoioun*, "the Spirit is the thing making alive..." (Jn 6:36).

Still another verb, *zao*, means "to live" or "to be alive." In his Eucharistic Discourse, John compares the life which Jesus has in the Father to the life of the Christian partaking of the Eucharistic bread. His Jesus says *zo dia ton patera*, "I live because of the Father," and thus *ho trogon me kakeinos zesei di eme*, "the one eating me, even that one will live because of me" (Jn 6:57). Jesus' unbegotten existence springs eternally from the Father's life: our life as Christians is maintained in the same way when we share in the Eucharist, our source of new life. "If you do not eat the flesh of the Son of Man...*ouk echete zoen en eautois*, you have not life in yourselves" (Jn 6:53).

The point is that *zoe* is not something that humanity has of its own nature. Humanity by its own nature has *bios*, and can only be raised to *zoe* by participating in Jesus' own *zoe*, which Jesus himself draws from the Father.

A Closer Look
at the Language

We should first note that the Greek language used in the
New Testament is not the same as that spoken by the people
of Greece today. Nor is it the same as that spoken by
Socrates five centuries before Jesus' time. The Greek used in
the New Testament is *Koine* ("common") Greek, a form of
the Greek language which developed roughly 300 years
before Jesus' time.

Koine Greek was the pidgin English of the time, a form
of Greek used by people whose principal language was
something else. Jesus' native tongue, for example, was
Aramaic. Many people in Jesus' day needed to speak Greek
as a secondary language in order to communicate in the
largely Greek-speaking world of the ancient Middle East.

Let's look at some *Koine* Greek expressions: *he basilissa*
("the queen"), *ho neanias* ("the young man"), *to ergon* ("the
work").

Immediately we notice something about Greek that is
different from English. In English if we say "the queen," "the
young man," or "the work," the definite article *the* doesn't
change its spelling. In Greek, however, the definite article
changes according to the *gender* of the word it modifies.
Thus the feminine for *the* in this instance is spelled (oddly
enough) *he*, the masculine is *ho* and the neuter *to*. All three
words means *the*, but their spelling and pronunciation change
to fit the gender of the word which they modify.

Not only that, the spelling of a noun can itself change
depending on its use in a particular sentence, just as
pronouns do in English. If I wanted to say "the queen's
work" in Greek, I would say *to ergon tes basilisses*, which

133

means the work *of* the queen. Notice that *to* and *ergon* ("the work") are spelled just as before, but that the spelling of "the queen" is now changed. That is because it is now used in another *case*, the genitive case, which denotes possession (like the pronoun *her*). Virtually every time a Greek word is used in a different case its spelling (and the spelling of the preceding *the*) changes.

For example, when I say "I love God" in Greek, the word *God* reads *ton Theon* ("the God"). If I say "the word *of* God," the spelling changes to *"tou Theou"* ("of the God"). This characteristic of the language explains why you found the same Greek word spelled differently in different contexts in the preceding pages.

This propensity for Greek words to change their spelling can sometimes cause confusion. For example, if I say "she does so-and-so," I would use for "she" the word *aute* (pronounced "ought-ay"). If I say "this queen," I use the same word *aute* to modify *basilissa*. In effect, then, *aute* means both "she" and "this." (The problem is resolved in Greek by the use of different accent marks.) Further, even numbers change their spelling in Greek. "One young man" is *eis neanias*, while "one queen" is *mia basilissa*.

By far the most difficult problem caused by these changes in spelling concerns the Greek *verbs*. Greek values the *sound* of a word more than it does rigid spelling rules, and will therefore often completely change the spelling of a word just to make the word sound more euphonious. One verb can have nearly 500 different endings and prefixes! By the time a verb's spelling is adjusted to suit the sound in the complicated form like "let such-and-such happen to us," the verb may no longer look anything like its simple form of "I do such-and-such." Let's illustrate this by looking first at an "easy" verb, and then at a few mind-bogglers.

"Believe" is a verb that's regular throughout. "I believe" is *pisteuo*. "I believed" is *episteusa*, a little different in spelling but still recognizable. "I shall believe" is *pisteuso*, again, fairly easy to identify as part of the same family.

Now, however, consider the verb *call*. The present tense ("I call") is *kaleo*. Because of certain Greek pronunciation

134

rules which we needn't go into here, "I was called" is spelled *eklethen* and "I will be called" *klethesomai*—neither of which immediately informs us that we are dealing with *kaleo*. Or take *open: anoigo* is "I open," *eneochthe* "I am opened." Further examples needn't detain us. You can see by now that Greek verbs can be very difficult to identify, and thus to translate.

Another hardship for the translator is the word order of a Greek sentence. A different arrangement of the words can alter the meaning. For example, *ho agathos anthropos* means "the good man," while *agathos ho anthropos* means "the man is good." (The Greek usually omits *is* in such a situation.) Further, where we would say, "The woman writes a good letter," the same sentence in Greek would correctly read, "The a writes woman letter good."

To make things worse, there is no hard and fast rule in Greek for the order of words. Greek is prone to *great* variation in its word order. For example, "The axe lies at the root of the trees" (Mt 3.10) is, in the Greek, "The axe at the root of the trees is laid." In the clause "If a man keeps your word he will never taste death" (Jn 8:52), the Greek order is, "If anyone the word of me keeps, by no means will he taste of death unto the age."

These are just a few tidbits to keep in mind. Before concluding, let's sample a few Greek sentences. I'll let you straighten out the word order where necessary by checking the Scripture references I've provided.

(1) Jn 14:6: *"ego eimi he hodos kai he aletheia kai he zoe."* ("I am the way and the truth and the life.")

(2) Jas 2:26: *to soma choris pneumatos nekron estin.* (The body without spirit dead is.)

(3) Jn 10:11: *"ego eimi ho poimen ho kalos."* ("I am the shepherd the good.")

(4) Jn 15:1: *"ego eimi he ampelos he alethine, kai ho pater mou ho georgos estin.* ("I am the vine the true, and the father of me the vinedresser is.")

(5) 1 Cor 1:25: *to asthenes to Theou ischuroterou ton anthropon.* (The weakness of the God is stronger than the men.)

(6) Jn 2:1: *kai en he meter tou Iesou ekei.* (And was the mother of the Jesus there.)

(7) Mt 16:18: *"su ei Petros, kai epi taute te petra oikodomeso mou ten ekklesian."* ("You are Peter, and on this the rock I will build of me the church.")

(8) Jn 19:22: *apekrithe ho Pilatos "ho gegrapha, gegrapha."* (Answered the Pilate: "What I have written, I have written.")

(9) Mt 6:11: *"ton arton hemon ton epiousion dos hemin semeron."* Lk 11:3: *"ton arton hemon ton epiousion didou hemin to kath hemeran."* ("The bread of us the daily give us to each day.")

(10) Mt 26:26b: *"labete phagete touto estin to soma mou."* "Take, eat: this is the body of me.")

The Greek Alphabet

α (alpha)   as in father
β (beta)   as in beach
γ (gamma)   as in gun
δ (delta)   as in daisy
ε (epsilon) as in met
ζ (zeta)   as in ads
η (eta)   as in they
θ (theta)   as in thin
ι (iota)   as in sit, and also sing
κ (kappa)   as in king
λ (lambda)   as in loop
μ (mu)   as in me
ν (nu)   as in new
ξ (xi)   as in asks
ο (omicron) as in log
π (pi)   as in pie
ρ (rho)   as in rhyme
σ (sigma)   as in stew
τ (tau)   as in tea
υ (upsilon) as in ewe
φ (phi)   as in phone
χ (chi)   as in chiropractor
ψ (psi)   as in upsets
ω (omega)   as in old

Locater Chart

Index

Scripture Index

144